The King
of the Cats

Farrar, Straus
and Giroux
New York

"The King of the Cats" and other remarks on writers and writing

by F. W. Dupee

In Memoriam
Richard Chase 1914-1963

Foreword

With few exceptions the essays and reviews here brought together were originally written for periodicals during the past fifteen years. They have all been much revised and, in some cases, re-titled. I have omitted from the list any extended comment on certain writers (for example Hemingway, Faulkner and Norman Mailer) about whom a profusion of recent criticism already exists in book form. I have given precedence to one type of literary journalism that seemed to me rather neglected when, some ten years ago, I first became aware of its possibilities for me. This is the type that I here call the "literary portrait." Based upon volumes of biography, letters and memoirs, the literary portrait is of course an old form of critical comment. Highly developed in the last century by such writers as Sainte-Beuve and Macaulay, it has not altogether lacked practitioners in the present century, one of them being Edmund Wilson. Naturally I do not pretend that literary portraiture is superior to, or a substitute for, good criticism of a more orthodox kind. I have attempted it only because, as I say, it seemed relatively uncommon in our time and because, for whatever psychological reasons, it has proved attractive to me personally.

No doubt this volume as a whole will strike some readers

as deplorably miscellaneous. Again, I can only plead that I
have *liked* being miscellaneous, at whatever cost to outward
consistency and inward commitment. I can best explain my
liking for it by quoting from a memorial essay on André Gide
that I wrote for the *Columbia Review* in 1951, the year of
Gide's death. The essay as a whole has not seemed to me
worth reprinting in this volume. The parts of it that defined
Gide's idea of culture, as I understood it, do however correspond to what I think my own convictions on the subject are
—allowing for all possible differences between Gide's mind
and accomplishments and mine. The passage also suggests,
perhaps, the extent to which his example, together with those
of H. L. Mencken, the early T. S. Eliot, Edmund Wilson and
other writers closer to home, helped me to piece together,
years ago, a conception of culture and of criticism which I
have tried in some measure to sustain through the decades:

André Gide did not often talk of culture in a theoretical
way; and he never talked, as so many have done in our disrupted age, of the attractions of a *homogeneous* culture. He
was conspicuous by the fact that the word "unity," save as
a principle of art, had no power to captivate his imagination.
If a kind of ideal of cultivation did emerge out of his life and
writings and the long guerilla warfare of his ideas, it remained largely unformulated; above all, it was never projected nostalgically on the past or dogmatically on the future.
It perhaps only amounted to what a gifted man, or body of
such men, could accomplish for himself or themselves by
way of the discovery of truth and the creation of beauty
in any stage of culture short of barbarism. Gide was not, in
my opinion, among the greatest artists of his time. The great
poems and novels were written, in many cases, by the very

men who dreamed of homogeneous societies: Rilke, Eliot, Yeats, Proust. It remained for Gide to make explicit, and to make *exciting*, the minimum faith, the practical faith in self, by which they all necessarily lived and wrote, and without which they would have been helpless.

Hence his own tireless habit of self-cultivation. In this respect he had always a frankly exalted and exploratory air, like that of a young man proudly getting up on subjects not included in the curriculum and reading Villon in the train. It is true that his moral ideas led a life of their own and did not exist merely to subserve his general culture. Yet they had a distinct bearing on it; even the extreme individualism and diabolism of his earlier years were a way of saying, as Henry James had said in his milder way, that culture was founded in experience, that experience begins with a knowledge of good and evil, and that knowledge is always primarily personal. Nor is it to impugn Gide's authority as an artist to suggest that his writing of tales and plays was itself entirely continuous with his other acts of self-cultivation: his incessant reading, his study of languages, his making of translations and anthologies, his editing and travelling and piano-playing and gardening, his pleasure in botany and entomology. He was a good artist in proportion as he was a good amateur— and in being so he helped to rehabilitate that word *amateur*, which has been made disreputable by the modern pride in pure creation and unremitting professionalism.

Contents

Literary
Portraits

The
Other
Dickens

In our time Dickens has been as thoroughly rediscovered as any writer of the past—assuming that he was ever really lost to view. His major novels are all once more in print, supplied with painstaking introductions by some of the best critics. In "Dickens: The Two Scrooges," Edmund Wilson has devoted to him one of his finest psychological studies; and Edgar Johnson's two-volume Life, *Charles Dickens: His Tragedy and Triumph,* is the definitive work in its field and a classic of modern biography. Only Dickens's letters have remained inaccessible, save in old, untrustworthy, out-of-print editions or in an enormous, expensive, out-of-print edition of more recent date. An exception is *The Heart of Charles Dickens,* the volume that Professor Johnson has made from Dickens's letters to Angela Burdett-Coutts. But these are his communications to a rather special lady with whom he had a rather special relationship. Meanwhile, in the bulk and variety of his labors as a correspondent Dickens made a great contribution to epistolary literature. His genius—as writer, friend, and public man—informs most of his letters, from the confident opening lines to the confident signature.

It was a remarkable signature for those days of emphatic identities asserted in fancy penmanship. The assertion of identity was emphatic but the penmanship was not fancy. It said CHARLES DICKENS in large, easily legible characters; and when there was space left on the page, the pen tended to race on, filling it with a long kite-tail of a flourish. In those free, full, unembarrassed transfusions of personality that were Dickens's letters, even the flourish seemed to say something. One could read in it a reluctance to finish, a promise of more to come, a sort of "to be continued" such as he appended to the successive installments of his serially published novels. One of the incidental attractions of the letters is that they are rather different in spirit—we shall presently see how—from the novels. Yet they obviously owe some of their disciplined spontaneity to their origin in a mind habituated to ready communication, affectionately conscious of an affectionate audience, aware that its productions were being eagerly waited for. No doubt this awareness sometimes weighed heavily on Dickens as a correspondent. He was a prodigy of good will and fluency, not a monster of them, and he could be perfunctory, slightly impatient, apologetic for lapses and delays, like anybody else. One acquaintance living in Lausanne seems to have expected him to report periodically on world affairs. This man inspired the only dull sequence of letters Dickens wrote.

For the rest, the promise of more to come was generally fulfilled with the expected liveliness. He wrote to a number of friends through long, formidably busy years; while the unknown admirer of his work or petitioner for his charity was reasonably certain to get a reply that was charming, thoughtful and believable beyond the call of duty. For Dickens made duty a pleasure if anyone ever did, and as a correspondent it was his pleasure to breathe amiability upon what he knew to be an unlovely world. His letters were acts of friendship, even when they were about business. Any claims

they have on literature are primarily based on this consideration. He wrote them to further human intercourse, not to
further the art of letter-writing as such. Whatever thoughts
he may have had of posterity were probably attended by the
hope that posterity would be disappointed. He made bonfires
of the letters that came to him from others; and if he failed to
ask that all of his own be destroyed in turn, it was doubtless
from common sense. They were too numerous, too far-flung.
Sitting down to his correspondence nearly every day of his
life, when his literary work for that day was done, he wrote
as many as twelve letters at a stretch and sent them off just
about everywhere. Only a bonfire on a world scale could
have destroyed the letters of Charles Dickens.

His correspondents naturally tended to preserve them and
they survive today by the thousands. The known or sus-
pected losses in their ranks are few. These include the letters
he wrote to Ellen Ternan, his mistress in his last years, which
exist so far only in rumor; and those parts of his letters to
John Forster that Forster disposed of after pasting the other,
and doubtless more significant parts, in the manuscript of his
Life of Charles Dickens. In the largest collection of Dickens's
letters to date, that of the Nonesuch edition of his work, they
fill three tall volumes of some nine hundred pages each, and
the projected Pilgrim edition of them will probably be larger
by several volumes.

Their very abundance is one of the essential characteristics of Dickens's letters. Without it they would not be that
"*auto-biography,* unrivaled in clearness and credibility,"
which Carlyle said they were. They would not be "in themselves a life work," as Lionel Trilling says they are. Dickens's
letters are a life work in themselves because they are distinct
in bulk and, as noted above, partly distinct in spirit from his

life work as a novelist, while being in their lesser way comparable to the novels in scope and quality. Their scope is Dickens's scope as the most popular good writer of his day and the master of his age in many of its extra-literary aspects. Their quality is his quality as a man and is as plain to see as it is intricate in its manifestations and causes.

A man of action if any literary man ever was, he writes his letters not as a spectator of events but as one who is in the thick of them. Indeed he is best at reporting events of his own making, and these were spectacular enough. Certain occasions excepted, he is no such social observer as Horace Walpole and Henry Adams are in their letters. Of affairs beyond his reach he is a diffident, even impatient, chronicler, unless he can project himself into them by some feat of comic fantasy. This he does, for example, in the case of Queen Victoria's marriage, which he proposes to prevent by storming the palace and carrying her off like Lochinvar; or in that of the Crystal Palace exposition, where a tale told of a little boy lost at the exposition and wandering out into London under the impression that he is still inside the grounds contains the writer's whole exasperated response to that famous showing of the trophies of human progress.

Dickens is a man of action for whom the troubled, often fruitless, distinctions between art and action, artist and man, artist and non-artist scarcely exist. His whole personal history works against them. His vocation for literature follows naturally, if by no means inevitably, from his youthful occupation as a reporter. He continues to identify that vocation with a regular trade or profession; and he labors to enhance its dignity in a society that is far from generous in granting dignity to the unestablished, whether persons or classes or professions. The society's cruel exclusiveness is hateful to him; yet he strives to establish himself and his fellow writers in it on their own terms.

In all this Dickens's passion for justice is inflamed by an undying sense of outrage which had its beginnings in the now famous ordeal of his boyhood. The distress of the twelve-year-old boy who saw his father suddenly imprisoned for debt and was himself made to drudge long hours in the unaccustomed squalor of a shoe-blacking plant lives on in the mature Dickens, although he confides these facts to John Forster alone. Indeed the events of his twelfth year seem to have constituted one of those family crises that cast their shadow back over the family's past and forward over its future. For young Dickens it was a crisis of the affections as well as a crisis in the Dickenses' social history. A nestling suddenly thrust from the nest, he never quite forgave his mother for her seeming indifference to his sufferings in the blacking plant. Grown up and married, he tends to visit his suspicions and resentments on his own wife, who, aided no doubt by her intrinsic faults, is finally made to re-enact the essentials of the mother's failure: she too is "apathetic" (his word) towards *their* children.

At the same time he has fears for the social well-being of the family. His paternal grandparents were domestic servants; and although his father, John Dickens, succeeded in extricating himself from that class—he was first a government employee, then a journalist of sorts—he was given to improvidence as to a kind of fate. There is reason to guess that he was morally unequal to his improved social position, remaining always in a state of partial dependency on others and his genial fecklessness turned into an ungenial, even criminal, parasitism in two of Charles Dickens's brothers. Hence Dickens's tremendous will to power, to success in the

world, to respectability; and hence his affinity with another
active type of his century (and ours), a type more ambitious
than the craftsman or professional. Dickens is the artist as
tycoon, dedicated to building up an impregnable personal
empire, literary, domestic, and financial. His ambition throbs
unmistakably in his letters. Like our Victorian grandfathers
whose sense of power was manifested in their weighty tread
on the floor, their heavily drawn breaths, their loudly ticking
watches, Dickens is almost physically present in the assured
rhythms and turns of speech of his epistolary prose. He
knows, as he confides to his wife, "what a thing it is to
have power." Yet his sense of power is infinitely refined by its
supreme confidence in itself, in short by his consciousness of
genius; and his greatness, unlike that of the legendary tycoon, is of the proudly accommodating kind. Much of the
legendary life of that type is nevertheless in evidence in his
letters. Three times he and his family make that significant
move which Hardy will describe in one of his great poems.

> They change to a high new house,
> He, she, all of them—aye,
> Clocks and carpets and chairs
>   On the lawn all day . . .

Three times the Dickenses move, each time to a higher
house. Indeed, no ordinary tycoon cared more for clocks and
carpets and chairs—or mirrors and curtains and stairs—than
Dickens does. In his householding capacity he combines the
scruples of an ambitious hostess with the vigilance of a con-
cierge. His passion for domestic order equals his sense of
power but can seem more oppressive, for it often appears to
operate at the expense of his wife. Poor "apathetic" incompetent Catherine Dickens, so tactless in company, so given to

misdirecting letters, turning her ankle, falling through trap-doors on stages, dropping her bracelets in the soup—she is definitely not to be trusted as a householder. When he proposes to bring a guest home for the week end he must tell her to arrange the guest's room in such and such a manner and lay out a copy of the newly published *Scarlet Letter* for him to read (the guest is a judge).

Yet Dickens has real cause for anxiety in these respects. With his large and clamoring body of dependents, including the ten children that the listless but ineluctably fertile Catherine bears him, he is often a very put-upon man, a condition he supports with amazing humor, fortitude and cleverness. But he doesn't merely support this life; he turns it into elaborate gaiety with his inventive parties, games, theatricals, pet names. And if he generally adheres to the type of the tycoon, like Scott, the elder Dumas, Mark Twain and other writers of the nineteenth century, he avoids what was often their fate. His unsuccessful ventures are few and he never knows the ultimate Victorian disgrace of a bankruptcy.

This triumphant man of action naturally admires the active virtues and suspects the passive ones. "What a long time he is, growing up," Dickens remarks with dry indulgence about his father. "Manly," meaning what we mean by "mature," is a favorite word of praise with him; and his passion for maturity helps to determine the moral atmosphere of his letters. It is, however, an atmosphere in which the *style* of a deed, the tact or humor or pride that goes into its performance, contributes much to its value. In his feeling for the aesthetics of conduct he is not to be surpassed by Henry James. And in his moral sense the Dickens of the letters is more urbane, sinuous, experimental than the reader of his novels might expect him to be. Where the novelist is often instinc-

tively identified with the stark taboos and inclusive judgments of the folk mind of his time, the letter-writer draws his
standards more from his daily experience in the world, often
ignoring the taboos, judging people according to their merits
as individuals, or simply suspending judgment. The very
firmness of his literary bond with the popular morality allows him a large liberty when it comes to particular cases.
The Victorian smugness—there are other kinds—which in its
sheer excess of feeling advertises an uneasy relation to the
popular morality, is alien to Dickens. He probably could not
write what Thackeray wrote to his mother, speaking of *Vil-
lette:* "I don't make my *good* women ready to fall in love
with two men at once." Nor would he, in all likelihood,
simply *refuse* to read the notorious Balzac, as George Eliot
refused to do.

Sometimes Dickens appears to be surprised by his own
susceptibility. During one of his philanthropic ventures he
encounters a young woman whom circumstances have forced
into genteel prostitution and who yet enjoys the love and respect of her brother and even humbly respects herself—"respects" is of course the key word and it is Dickens's. Her life,
he asserts, is "a romance so astonishing and yet so intelligible
as I never had the boldness to think of." It is: sexual vice is
incompatible with respect and love in the world of his novels. Indeed Dickens's personal story as it appears in his letters must itself often seem a romance that he never thought
of as a writer. It is a romance in which, for example, a nobleman (the Duke of Devonshire) can be really noble and a
woman with a past (Lady Blessington) can be completely
charming. It is a romance, too, in which the poor and the
oppressed can arouse his unqualified ire, even when they are
acting out of the very exigencies of their condition. This the

unfortunate baker's man learns when he is caught urinating on Dickens's gate, is threatened with the Police Act by the great humanitarian himself, and can only demand to know, as Dickens reports, "what I should do 'if I was him.'" It is a romance, finally, in which the rhythms of existence itself are indifferent to moral impulses. Here Time alone is the great force for change and no one is hustled to his destiny by any patrol wagon of a plot. As distinguished from the characters in his novels, his acquaintances merely alter with the years, for better and worse, as people do in what we call "life" and in novels of the kind Dickens didn't write.

The differences are, however, far from absolute. Especially at moments of great emotional stress is the novelist firmly reunited with the letter-writer. The impulse of melodrama breaks out in him in the fierce accusations and final judgments he brings to the affair of his separation from his wife. On the other hand, his extravagantly idealizing tendency makes an unmitigated heroine of Mary Hogarth, his dead sister-in-law, as it does of the Little Nells and Esther Summersons of his novels.

Readers of Dickens's letters breathe not only an intriguing moral air but an exhilarating air of vast public acclaim. As between Dickens and his public, the acclaim is seen to be intensely heady, richly earned, cheerfully given, cheerfully accepted. Originating with the success of *The Pickwick Papers*, his fame is sustained by his continued performance as a novelist and by his other brilliant activities. The fame follows him all his days like a brass band and can be heard sounding from the distant square even when he is in seclusion. Indeed it has the peculiar interest of seeming to exceed its natural causes, as poetry does, or what is called "grace." A self-enhancing sort of fame, a celebrated celebrity, it is the kind of thing that people of all classes and tastes enjoy participating in. Dickens is the man you love to love, as Charlie Chaplin will be in his heyday, only Dickens is far more so. And Dickens never has a heyday followed by a fall from grace of the sort that often occurs in these situations. When opposition threatens, as it frequently does, especially in the easily stampeded American public which he confronts during his two stormy tours of the United States, he knows how to defy it and make it work for him. The band music never turns to jeers and never really stops.

His reporting of his exploits, in his letters, is a triumph of what I have called his accommodating pride. No other hero has ever made the life of heroism more attractive, more believable. Mere modesty is as foreign to him as mere vanity. He can delight in his fame without either exaggerating it or diminishing it, and his friends can become naturalized citizens of his privileged world without forfeiting their sense of the privilege. Sharing the pleasures of his celebrity with his correspondents, he is able to avoid the nemesis of egotism. The Dickens of the letters is superstitious in the profound way that other great men of action have been superstitious. Rarely does he announce any plan without adding "God willing," as if intent on appeasing a still greater planmaker than himself. So too with the news he gives his correspondents of his feats as a writer, actor, reader from his works, party giver, or whatever. He takes the curse off his ego by splitting his ego up. There is the Charles Dickens who writes the letters and there is "the inimitable Boz," that convenient alter-ego early bestowed on him by a former teacher. Dickens becomes, along with his friends, the fascinated observer of this phenomenal homunculus of a Boz. Boz can do anything. If he starts to break down under the strain, just feed him a dozen oysters and a pint of champagne and he will bounce back. Boz acts; Dickens watches, enjoys, and records the results in his letters. This process makes for accuracy as well as detachment on the letter-writer's part. The creator of the fantastic Mrs. Gamp and the fantastic Circumlocution Office is able to convey the assurance that he doesn't fancify facts in his letters. Nor do the facts require embroidering; they are fantastic in themselves.

With the years his fame only increases, reaching a high point when at last he takes to the road as a reader from his works, face to face with his tumultuous public. Meanwhile the letters testify to a counter-development in him, a growing consciousness of his inner self and its unappeasable desires. The "one happiness I have missed in life" begins to haunt him and make him fearfully restless. The one happiness is several things: sex, easy companionship, freedom from the self-imposed restraints of his impregnable personal empire, freedom to write in defiance of the Victorian taboos that he himself has done much to establish. All of these and more: he comes to know the intrinsic sense of loss that is common to the supreme genius who is exhausting the possibilities of his culture, of his very condition as a human being. Dickens does not respond to this tragic process as Tolstoy will do, by a mental flight, magnificent and quixotic, into the infinite. A man of action to the end, Dickens meets the situation as he can—by putting his wife away, secretly taking a mistress, going on the road, amassing still more fame and money. On the question of literary freedom he is assailed by an angry incoherence that is quite untypical of him. He blames the English morality, blames those who find fault with it, and does nothing except to avail himself more and more of the greater personal freedom of Paris. *His* flight is limited by geography; and the scrutiny of his inner self, carried on in letters to Forster and others, has comparable limits. He undertakes it not as one who makes a practice of introspection but as one who is driven to it by a great need and rises gallantly to the occasion. Thus the risks run by the *confirmed* introspective are, at least, not Dickens's risks. He is in no danger of talking himself morosely and glibly out of existence. In his unprecedented—for him—confession to Maria Winter, despite all the sad things he confesses to, there is the exhilaration of discovery, the freshness of a relatively untried passion and idiom.

His pleasure in friendship never lessens, however, and he adds to the sum of his acquaintances the rather racy and adventurous—one gathers—Wilkie Collins, his occasional companion in Paris and Italy. Friendship is Dickens's natural medium as a man. It remains generally unthreatened by the fierce demands he often makes upon his domestic intimates. He is obviously not a virtuoso of love but he is a virtuoso of friendship, practicing his art on all comers and thus transfiguring—as far as anyone can—the dreary realities of strife and boredom. But it is no improbable idyl of friendship that the letters record. His amiability can turn into bitterness and even physical revulsion. Beneath his manly good will, his hearty toleration of people, there is an aching fastidiousness. From egotism in its many guises he recoils exactly as he does in his novels, such vices manifesting themselves for him in deformities of body and speech. "The shape of his head (I see it now) was misery to me, and weighed me down in my youth," he says of Lord Grey, the statesman whom the young Dickens, as a reporter in the Parliament, had seen and heard too much of. So there is in the letters news of quarrels; and Dickens occasionally criticizes the people who are closest to him, complaining of Forster's loudness of speech and mildly caricaturing Collins's pretentious chatter about the arts. But there is a taboo on criticism for its own sake, and malice is definitely banned. Good will prevails, and not only for reasons of conscience. The friends addressed in Dickens's letters have a way of being more than friends in the abstract. He likes to put them to work, to associate them with him in various enterprises that redound to their common good and pleasure. John Forster is not only his intimate friend but his literary counselor and, on occasion, his collaborator in the financing and editing of periodicals. Forster is a special case of a general rule. Dickens involves others in his elaborate theatricals, interests them in his philanthropies, makes them contributors to his periodicals, engages them in strenuous well-planned excursions. A visit to the Honorable Richard Watson of Rockingham Castle is apt to center on the production of a play, with all present taking parts. Friendship may sometimes be tried by such exertions but it is kept from languishing. This Victorian Falstaff embroils almost everyone in his intricate frolics and as a result almost everyone shows unsuspected talent, helping the company to earn large sums for charity and to make the Queen laugh—she will not be excluded from the revels.

In most cases, it is true, his close friends are the kind of people who can profit from such exercises. Dickens's immediate circle consists of journalists like Douglas Jerrold, Mark Lemon and W. H. Wills, men of the theater like W. C. Macready, popular artists and illustrators like Daniel Maclise and Clarkson Stanfield, fellow novelists of wide appeal like Collins and Bulwer-Lytton. With all their differences and their often prominent egos, they have by trade or temperament a common accessibility to the gregarious London life and the resounding public occasion. This does not keep some of them from enjoying a high degree of intimacy with Dickens. Forster and Collins obviously share his confidences and know his opinions on most subjects. It is not in any of them, however, to be to Dickens what, say, Schiller was to Goethe, or George Sand to Flaubert, or Hawthorne to Melville. Evidently it is not in Dickens to require friends and correspondents of this stature, and the absence of them is doubtless felt as a loss to his letters considered as literary documents. He is often discriminating in what he says about works of literature, including his own works. But he is best in his powerful feeling for the general responsibilities and privileges of the literary *profession*. He is untempted by those further reaches of thought which, for many writers, make the exchange of letters with their peers an adventure and a necessity.

The power of thought displayed in his letters is of quite another kind. It springs from his concentration upon the world of actual experience, above all the world of social experience, as he knows it in the mid-nineteenth century. The imposition of a new industrial order on a feudal order of long standing throws that world into confusion, misery and fear— a fear of revolution comparable in its intensity to the fear of atomic extinction pervading our own mid-century; and Dickens's mind is constantly harassed and exercised by the distressing spectacle. But he takes thought of the abuses only with the intention of taking action against them. The *habit* of reform, which afflicts others of his time and will afflict even Bernard Shaw, is absent from Dickens's temperament. In his letters he denounces the abuses rather less often than we might expect of so famous a champion of the unfortunate. He is too busy with his practical attempts at reform to devote much passion to their manifestations and causes. It is during his first tour of the United States, where he is not only greatly disappointed but—as a foreigner—relatively helpless to do anything, that he is most fiercely and consistently the social observer. In America, therefore, the essential concern of all his criticism becomes unmistakably clear. It is directed chiefly against the failures of intelligence, courage and feeling in individuals. Whether he is assailing the new practice of solitary confinement in American prisons, or the tendency to conformity among American writers, or the national love of boasting and snooping, Dickens usually comes down to the problems of personality and the well-being of the single separate person, including the artist. "*You* live here, Macready, as I have sometimes heard you imagining!" he writes from Baltimore in 1842. "Macready, if I had been born here and had written my books in this country, producing them with no stamp of approval from other lands, it is my solemn belief that I should have lived and died poor, unnoticed, and a 'black sheep' to boot."

True, Dickens's name has become a byword for the reforming artist. Yet there is in all his letters, I think, no mention of an abuse, from the Ragged Schools to the pirating practices of editors, that the most ardent conservative of our own day would not find intolerable, an invasion not merely of the "rights" but of the bases of personality. In this way Dickens remains the friend of the race as well as of his numerous correspondents; and it is to the race that his letters, careless though he was of their future, finally belong.

1960

Sir Richard
and
Ruffian Dick

In high school a friend and I sometimes managed to get hold of the various volumes of *The Arabian Nights* in the privately printed translation by Richard Burton. There we found greater wonders than any in "Aladdin and His Lamp" and other expurgated or inauthentic examples of oriental story that had reached us as children. In Burton's "Terminal Essay" to the *Nights,* when we had the luck to get it also, were still better things, true things in plain prose with a minimum of Latin. How is it possible for a sodomite Moslem prince to force a Christian missionary against his will and the strong resistance instinctively put up by his sphincter muscle? Burton could tell us: by the judicious use of a tent peg. Not that we had really wondered about such things. Burton's attraction was that he set the questions as well as answered them, enlarging our curiosity even while he satisfied it—the perfect pedagogue. There was much also in the "Terminal Essay" to inflame the anti-Victorian passions we were beginning to feel. The Victorian age, Burton said, was "saturated with cant and hypocrisy." We knew that already but were always glad to hear it said again. But I doubt that we knew anything about the other exploits for which he had once been famous: his pilgrimage, in Moslem disguise, to Mecca; his expedition to the still more forbidden city of Harrar; his discovery of Lake Tanganyika, an adventure that inspired Livingstone and Stanley and helped to clear up the ancient mystery surrounding the sources of the Nile. It seems unlikely that we knew how very recently he had died (in 1890).

A revival of Burton in all his aspects appears a possibility at present. His translations of the *Kama Sutra* and *The Perfumed Garden,* those cheerful excursions into sexual physiology, have circulated both in hard covers and in paperback. Three new accounts of his career have come out in the recent years. Two of them (*That Blackguard Burton,* by Alfred Bercovici, and *Death Rides a Camel,* by Allen Edwardes) are potboilers; but the third, *Burton, A Biography of Sir Richard Francis Burton,* by Byron Farwell, is a thorough and conscientious book, chiefly factual, rarely reflective. Presumably the writers and publishers responsible for these books think of Burton as a timely subject. Is he by some chance a spiritual ancestor of the many who at present, and generally with reason, seek to accomplish a moral revolution, a "breakthrough" into realms of greater personal autonomy and sexual freedom? Possibly. There are old photographs of Burton —dark, beetle-browed, his left cheek deeply scarred where a Somali warrior had put a spear through it, his gaze intensified by what is surely the Evil Eye, his mustaches six inches long and good for twirling. Such photographs suggest those sometimes reproduced on the jackets of books by our scarier contemporaries, Fiedler or Mailer, their faces bearded, sweaty, hostile, furrowed with existential woe.

On the whole, though, it is a question whether Burton is an ancestor anyone would want to claim. On Mr. Farwell's evidence, he was a compulsive egocentric whose arrogance and xenophobia surpassed even those of the Baron de Charlus. Whether Burton was as large a bundle of vices as Proust's character was is not clear from this book, to which Mr. Farwell, an IBM executive stationed in Switzerland, brings an innocence that is in remarkable contrast to its subject (the book, unfortunately, is also innocent of footnotes). But rumors abound, flowing chiefly no doubt from such writings of Burton's as the "Terminal Essay," with its luxuriant account of the history and techniques of pederasty. And just as there can be little doubt that he "tried everything," so there is little doubt that his sexual interests were connected with, and largely subordinate to, his sadistic ones. Charlus merely liked to snub his inferiors and be beaten with chains. Burton's writings show him to have been fascinated with forms of torture, with the surgical processes of circumcision and castration, both of males and females; with the art of scalping as practiced by American Indians; with the size of the genitals of males and females and the degree of satisfaction or its opposite implied by their size (he was a great measurer of the sexual organs of obliging natives). What makes him so difficult a hero, however, is not his sexuality, hot or cold, but his insensate truculence, as of a human weapon in perpetual readiness to deliver. As such he provides a very good show. An extreme case of the aberrant Victorian, he can greatly fascinate, if nothing else. If there was ever an unlovable rogue before the heroes of *The Ginger Man* and *Look Back in Anger* it was Richard Burton.

It all began, possibly, when, aged about six, he was taken by the headmaster of his French school to watch the guillotining of a criminal. He seems to have remembered this and left some record of it, for Mr. Farwell is able to recount the incident in some detail. Anyway, Burton's career as a voyeur of the lurid and exotic was in motion. His parents were well

born and well-to-do and chose to lead a wandering life on the
Continent: Tours, Blois, Pisa, Siena, Rome, etc. In Naples,
Burton, now aged fifteen, was collecting for burial the
corpses of cholera victims in the streets and noting the curious phosphorescence the bodies gave off at night. Later,
an officer in the Bombay Native Infantry, he was inspecting
male brothels in Sind and submitting to the army authorities
a report on techniques and finances (boys cost more than
eunuchs). The report was unsolicited and unwelcome. A
man that interested in vice was assumed to be vicious himself in those pre-Kinsey days. Future promotions for Burton
were delayed, but lengthy leaves of absence were granted
him several times.

His absences bring us to another side of Richard Burton.
They were usually granted that he might pursue his study of
oriental languages. This, naturally, was a subject of considerable utility to the invading British, and Burton had a genius
and a passion for it. His delight in *any* learning acquired on
his own was extreme—he had despised Oxford during a brief
stay there and had got himself expelled. He was among the
chief of the Victorian autodidacts just as he was among the
most formidable eccentrics of the time, and the two roles
were perhaps in his case related. "Eccentricity is, in fact,
practical madness," V. S. Pritchett has said; it is resorted
to "by those who are secretly up to something shameful or
stupid or muddleheaded. And in England most of us are."
Burton was muddleheaded but not stupid. His instinct of self-
concealment, if he had one, took the form of a sheltering
bravado which was in turn inseparable from his public personality. It earned him the nicknames of "Ruffian Dick" and
"The White Negro" among his army messmates in India. At
home he was to enjoy the friendship of Milnes, Swinburne,

Frederick Hankey, and other participants in, or connoisseurs of, *le vice anglais* (the phrase was used by Burton for sodomy and later by Mario Praz in *The Romantic Agony* for sadism). Thus his eccentricity was not in any simple sense a stratagem of self-concealment. It expressed, at least in part, an organic independence of English manners. This independence had been fostered by the years he spent abroad as child and boy, years prolonged in substance by the ceaseless changes of residence and the ever larger opportunities for graver and graver mischief (whores, swordplay, pyromania, attempted descents into the crater of Vesuvius).

Burton, it seems, reacted against his English origins in proportion as his feckless English parents proved incapable of controlling him and his younger brother (later beaten into lifelong idiocy by natives during an elephant hunt in India). England, Burton maintained, was hopelessly "lower class"; Oxford, apart from the gypsies camped in Bagley Wood, was dull. His expressed detestation of England seems to have exceeded in intensity any possible cause except one: an inverted nostalgia on his part, the will to defy what he had been deprived of. Perhaps this was the secret which he sought to disguise by his "practical madness." If so, the disguise was almost literal. His dark looks were alarmingly conspicuous in England and gave rise to suspicions that he had gypsy blood himself.

His love of learning was genuine, whatever its causes. True, the rage for collecting facts and impressions was, with him, indiscriminate. Tolstoy says of Vronsky when, self-exiled in Florence with Anna Karenina, Vronsky begins to be bored: "He was a sensible man and a Russian and could not merely go around looking at things, like an Englishman." The titles of Burton's 29-odd books give an idea of the variety of things he looked at: they range from *Etruscan Bologna: A Study* to *Falconry in the Valley of the Indus* to *A Glance at the* [Oberammergau] *"Passion Play."* Yet he was the opposite of the idle tourist Tolstoy had in mind. His traveling and looking were forms of participation in the community life of places other than England, places of his own choosing. He learned languages by taking native mistresses or, possibly, minions; he perfected them by assuming native disguises and setting up as a shopkeeper in the souks. In India once he acquired several monkeys, dressed a female of the troupe in silks and pearl earrings, and lived with them all as with a wife and family, meanwhile studying monkey language. Among the adherents of Sufism, an esoteric Islamic sect, he attained high rank.

Not that Burton gives much evidence of *enjoying* foreign places and peoples. On the contrary. Only among the desert Bedouins was he the utopian traveler. He admired the Bedouins for their "radiant innate idealism," their feudal grace, discipline, and pride of clan. Even so, he left it to Doughty to celebrate the Bedouins in a masterpiece. For the rest he was as fault-finding a traveler as Sterne's Smellfungus had been, viewing native "filth" and "corruption" with the cold eye of European superiority. On the American plains he was disappointed because the Indians, failing to attack, robbed him of the chance to kill some. In his later years, as an explorer and a consular officer in Africa (he eventually left the army for the foreign office), Burton served imperialism as shrewdly as his divided soul would permit. To the King of Dahomey he took presents from Queen Victoria, calming the king's annoyance at her failure to include a carriage drawn by white chargers.

Such were the contradictions that worked like madness in

the brain of this England-hating Englishman, who seems at moments to have been invented by Evelyn Waugh. No doubt the contradictions hampered him at just the moment when he might have won real glory at home and ended up—where his wife tried unsuccessfully to install him after his death— in a Westminster Abbey tomb. The moment came when he reached Tanganyika after incredible toils and dangers. There he halted, overcome with more than fatigue: with hatred for his bearers, the jungle and his fellow explorer, John Hanning Speke. Thus Speke could continue north on his own and become the sole discoverer of Lake Victoria, a really important prize. Speke's exploit caused the honors to be split between them; and Burton's quarrels with Speke, and Speke's later suicide, left the biggest trophies for Livingstone and Stanley. There were advantages to working, as Livingstone and Stanley did, for the glory of God or England or both. Burton could really only work for his divided soul. Thus East Africa failed him, as the army had, and his public role declined to that of a consular officer in relatively minor posts: Fernando Po, Santos in Brazil, Damascus, Trieste. Even in these places his energy and curiosity remained intact, until, confined chiefly to England by old age, he would interrupt his insular excursions to look at—for example—a mushroom farm.

Meanwhile, Mr. Farwell's reader, who has been panting after Burton through many crowded pages, undergoes a sharp reversal of feeling. He grows as bored with it all as Vronsky was in Florence. At first Burton's curiosity set Burton in violent motion across the world; and to the reader, as doubtless to Burton, the world looked like an infinitely capacious and inviting stage for those gratuitous prowls. But the same world has ended by resembling some place of dull confinement wherein Burton is forever and vainly, as he himself remarks, "kicking against the pricks." His talent for vaporizing romance was equaled by his talent for shrinking space.

But his adventures had come to include less strenuous kinds. There was his marriage and there were his translations, notably of *The Arabian Nights*.

Writing came all too easily to him. His numerous books tended to expand into garrulous monologues interrupted by garrulous footnotes. Or so I gather from what Mr. Farwell says about them and from the little I have been able to read of them myself. Sometimes the prose lights up and a scene materializes out of the vapors diffused by the writer's insistent personality. Curiously, though, the voice seems frequently to be not his own. Frequently it is the voice of some great Victorian gusher, Carlyle or Ruskin, caught at the moment of its thinnest flow. And the voice scolds, as Henry James said Ruskin often did, "like an angry governess." Burton is always passing sentence; his court is in perpetual session; no allusion is too insignificant to escape judgment even when the judgment is favorable: "says Bacon with his normal sound sense." Thus, rebel though he is, Burton reproduces and magnifies the worst fault of Victorian writing, its sententiousness. But sometimes the voice is that of a Persian poet, or, more happily, of Homer: the fleets of covered wagons he saw on a trip to the Mormon country were, "these long winding trains, in early morning like lines of white cranes trooping slowly over the prairies" (quoted by Mr. Farwell). My own "judgments" on his books are tentative and may be misleading. There could be better books in the Burton canon than those I have seen. His *Arabian Nights* was momentous for other reasons than its prose, whose somewhat labored archaisms align it with the Lang, Leaf and Myers *Iliad* rather than with the selective and inventive archaism of

Arabia Deserta, Doughty's masterpiece. Burton certainly cribbed from John Payne's translation (1882-84), as Mr. Joseph Campbell charges in his *Portable Arabian Nights* and as Mr. Farwell admits. Still, Burton's version was inclusive, unexpurgated. Through his courage and that of his associates in the Kamashastra Society, an informal organization of eroticists, it reached a large public. The "Terminal Essay," reread in middle age, remains a fascinating monument to curiosity.

Burton's marriage to Isabel Arundell proved more durable than his monkey household. It was nevertheless a bizarre romance. She was the conventionally brought up daughter of a Catholic family whose forebears had been in England since the Conquest. While still a young girl, she says, she had been told by a gypsy that she would marry a very dark man named Burton. Still quite young, she met Richard Burton during one of his brief stays in Europe and was instantly smitten. After many years and few meetings and despite her mother's objections she married him. Isabel's persistence, which had probably brought about the marriage in the first place, made it last. There is little evidence that she was interesting except for the extremes to which she carried both her romantic silliness and her pious prudery. Her "Rules For My Guidance As a Wife" survive. One rule reads: "Attend much to his creature comforts; allow smoking or anything else; for if you do not, *somebody else will*." If nothing else linked this strange pair it was the capacity of each to embrace wildly antithetical impulses. Isabel probably drew strength from the tradition of the innocent girl who marries a rake to reform him. Perhaps Burton wanted at last to *be* reformed, a little.

Once married he tried to maintain a partly separate existence as a consul in West Africa. This failing, he accepted

Isabel's constant companionship, with few signs of discomfort. His erotomania pained her but she allowed it, as she did his smoking—so long as he was alive. It seems to have been through her efforts that his achievements were finally recognized by the Queen and he became Sir Richard. A rancorous lone wolf in so many instances, he was capable of great good nature with a few individuals. Stanley, one of these, wrote of him, "What a grand man! One of the great ones in England he might have been, if he had not been cursed with cynicism." He loved his parents, whose restlessness he had inherited and made a fantastic career of. Immediately following his death, Isabel signalized the triumph of Patient Grizzel over Ruffian Dick by burning all his papers. The task took her several days and the news of it made a scandal in London. She saw him buried in the graveyard of a Catholic church in Mortlake, a dingy London suburb. Over his grave she ordered erected a mass of marble carved to look like an Arab tent.

May every breakthrough artist of our time have as fitting a tomb. Yet Burton seems to me to have been our spiritual ancestor in only one respect and that a negative one. With him, as with some of us some of the time, the conquest of personal autonomy and sexual freedom was accompanied by a ferocious and boring egotism. Too much autonomy made him a kind of automaton of aggression and animal courage. The spectacle presented by his life, although certainly unique in the ingenuity of its wildness, and as "fabulous," almost, as *The Arabian Nights* itself, tends in the long run to make for weariness insofar as it doesn't make for laughs. It is now easy to see that he was not, alas, a free spirit, any more than Charlus is, and that he was not really in advance of his time but behind it. Burton was a displaced Regency Beau, an admirable enough type when *not* displaced, as he was, in Victorian England. As it was, his hatred of Victorian England was fatally counterbalanced by his desire to be a part of it on his own terms. As it was, the energy, confidence, curiosity, and courage of the age were his in sizable amounts, together with still more of its brutality and self-importance. He embodied all this with stunning finality and so remains a far from negligible figure, even though he may not merit the full revival treatment.

1964

Behrman's
Beerbohm

To judge by *The Spirit of St. Louis,* his book of reminiscences, Lindbergh managed not only to fly the Atlantic
alone but, while doing so, to remember in an orderly manner
the leading events of his past life; and when he came to write
The Spirit of St. Louis a quarter of a century later, he was
able to remember his memories. Lindbergh's feats of formidable recall and precise mental navigation are repeated on a
smaller scale in *Portrait of Max,* S. N. Behrman's book about
his encounters with Max Beerbohm between 1952 and 1956,
the year in which the celebrated wit and dandy, parodist and
caricaturist, died, at the age of eighty-four in Rapallo, Italy.

An example of Mr. Behrman's use of the Lindbergh
method occurs at the book's close. Beerbohm lies dying in
the Rapallo hospital and Mr. Behrman, taking his last look at
the old artist's memento-strewn house, is assailed by a variety of convenient recalls. "I went out and walked up the
steps to the terrace. It was flooded with sunlight. There I
remembered a line of Max's: 'The past is a work of art, free of
irrelevancies and loose ends.'" Even Lindbergh's remarkable
memory failed to yield apposite quotations.

But in *Portrait of Max,* this mnemonic device does serve,
however awkwardly, a useful purpose. The book is largely a

record of the talk that passed between Beerbohm and Mr. Behrman during Mr. Behrman's several visits to Rapallo, the scene of Beerbohm's more than forty years of genial exile and sociable seclusion. Good as the stream of talk generally is and deliciously as one floats along on it as first, it soon begins to close inexorably over one, making breathing difficult. Mr. Behrman evidently wants to keep the reader alive. He also aims to inform him about Beerbohm's writings and drawings, many of which have faded from the public consciousness and are available only in the better libraries. So he includes much comment of a lightly descriptive and interpretive kind. His aims are understandable, and in itself his comment is often witty and apt. He is superb at the perilous enterprise of translating Beerbohm's caricatures, with their essentially graphic perceptions, into words.

The comment is good then, but the mnemonic device by which it is insinuated takes its toll of one's nerves. The general effect it is intended to produce is, I suppose, one of bland immediacy and omniscience. It is the same effect that is aimed at in those *New Yorker* "Profiles" the writers of which undertake to conceal their grubby efforts as researchers and interviewers by saying, "So-and-so observed to a visitor . . ." or "So-and-so was heard to remark recently . . ." Surely, with so much excellent material on so unhackneyed a subject, Mr. Behrman could have afforded to present it more candidly and unfancily. And considering that Beerbohm was a noted scourge of the coy locutions and vain artifices of writers, one thinks that Mr. Behrman might better not have risked a posthumous grin from his subject.

If Behrman's *Portrait* resembles a *New Yorker* "Profile," that is because it originally *was* a *New Yorker* "Profile," though of an unusually lengthy and festive kind. But while reading the work in that form, and while re-reading it lately in book form (the book is beautiful, with many reproductions of the caricatures), I was constantly put off, not only by the use of the recall technique but by the author's general unwillingness to go beyond the urbanely reportorial and descriptive approach. This approach may be justified by the frankly limited functions of the usual "Profile," where all is suppressed that might impair the slick surface and sharp outline of the thing. But it seems unequal to the job of reconsidering an artist who so cordially invites reconsideration at this time.

To be sure, Miss Ellen Moers, in her thoroughly original book, *The Dandy,* devotes an admirable concluding chapter to Beerbohm. She is as careful as Mr. Behrman is to avoid overloading "the Incomparable Max" with comparisons or snowing him with significance. But Beerbohm did once advise the prospective author of a book about him to "compare me," and Miss Moers tactfully follows his advice. She relates him to her general subject, the tradition of dandyism, where in part he clearly belongs. She also points to certain aspects of his family background and personal character which, far from boring or confusing us, prove exquisitely enlightening. His peculiar valetudinarianism, his constant identification of himself with the European past, his ability to be very much a part of the English literary life of, roughly, 1895-1914 and yet to be profoundly detached from it all, as if he were living through some phase of literary history long finished—all this is briefly clarified by Miss Moers.

So too with the events of Beerbohm's later life, even though these are not dealt with directly in *The Dandy.* His retirement to Rapallo, his refusal not only of publicity but of certain simple animal comforts, his willingness to live on a small income rather than be televised for a three-thousand-dollar fee, or have his works collected in a Modern Library Giant, or see his novel *Zuleika Dobson* dramatized at the request of a New York actress who hoped to perform the principal role—these facts, lovingly detailed by Mr. Behrman, are somehow made to look gratuitously wonderful in his account. With Miss Moers's insights in mind, they fall more naturally into the pattern of Beerbohm's life and character. The wonder of his modesty and stoicism remains; but, seeming less gratuitous, it can be relished without any suggestions of impertinence. After all, Beerbohm's was simply the honesty of an honest man, the modest greatness of a man who was modestly great.

In short, Miss Moers is what Mr. Behrman probably wouldn't be on a bet: an historical critic. He quotes Beerbohm's "compare me" only to refuse the injunction while enthusiastically associating himself with Beerbohm's well-known diffidence toward critics and criticism. In fact he associates himself with his subject so thoroughly that the originally delightful relationship between them grows sticky. And with the loss of distance and perspective there is a loss in the matter of selection and discrimination. "Max's eye caught the season's first gardenia in the flower border. We stopped to admire it." We stop to admire everything about darling Max, from the routine humor of the story about how he lost status with the hall porter of a London club to the trite half-truths into which his literary opinions sometimes resolve themselves. (He was a satirist, not a critic.) What strangely happens before we are finished is that Beerbohm becomes more and more intimately associated with Behrman, instead of Behrman with Beerbohm. The portrait of the master threatens to turn into a portrait of the disciple. Finally, as the anecdotes continue to pile up, Beerbohm comes to resemble one of those people for whom, cursed as they are with the spectator's role, life is a succession of unrelated ironies, a tale told by a compulsive raconteur. At this stage, the Rapallo recluse is easily imagined as a fixture at our own Algonquin, the legendary gathering place of *The New Yorker* wits and worldlings.

He wasn't a fixture there, of course, however much the Algonquin wits may have thought of him as one of their masters. Nor am I at all sure that the Algonquin wits have really existed as such; they may be a fiction of the popular mind. But if they are real, Beerbohm was not one of them even in spirit. He was not committed to the spectator's role and to making it pay, in money or anecdotes. Mr. Behrman knows what he was and gives plentiful evidence of it. In all his best work he was an artist of a peculiarly pure and uncompromising kind. To a considerable extent, he was this in his stories and essays and in the parodies composing *A Christmas Garland,* which more than one of his victims thought a masterpiece. He was superlatively and uniquely an artist in those works of comic drawing for which the word "caricatures," though it contented him, may seem inadequate to us. Done always from memory, done again and again even when he was in retirement and many of the subjects were dead, drawn on the best stock for exhibition and publication, scribbled hastily in book margins or letters or on mere scraps, painted in fresco on the walls of his Rapallo house, these queens and princes and statesmen, these artists and writers and actors, form a united spectacle of brilliant and oppressive fatuity.

If any quality of vision is common to the many caricatures of Max Beerbohm, it is somehow connected with the abuse of power. This is not the abuse of *social* power, as in Daumier's caricatures of towering judges and cowering culprits. Nor is it, as in Saul Steinberg, the abuse of cultural power, whereby people become as enigmatically intricate and ugly as the vulgar displays of architecture and decor that surround them. In Beerbohm, curiously, there are no victims apart from the wielders of power themselves. They are, it seems, their own victims. Prince Edward is stood in the corner of a Windsor Castle room for his sins; but he is as fat from his indulgence of them as Queen Victoria, who stood him there, is fat from the practice of her virtues. (Mr. Behrman notes the family resemblance here as he notes so much else of value in the caricatures.) So too with the writers whom Beerbohm portrayed again and again, in different situations but as a rule with the same essential features. George Moore is dim and rabbity; he seems dim and rabbity from the effects of his own scurryings and pantings as of a writer eternally in search of a subject. A miniature Kipling, tooting a tin horn, is being dragged off his feet by a huge swaggering Britannia with whom he has linked arms; but it was Kipling, the jingo of the Boer War, who began the alarming courtship. In still another sketch, Beerbohm returns to England after a long absence to find Shaw still standing on his head; the posture is uncomfortable and one of Shaw's legs is sagging; but what keeps him in it except his own acrobatic will to power?

Behrman's Beerbohm has his annoying lapses, as anyone's Beerbohm probably must have. He often seems to be carefully acting a part that has been shrewdly written for him by this accomplished playwright. But he is still a wonder, a precious anomaly, at once great and small, easy to forget but delightful to remember.

1960

The
Secret
Life of
Edward Windsor

With their famous subject, the Duke of Windsor's memoirs, *A King's Story*, are inevitably absorbing. They are dense with detail, painstaking in their reconstruction of the past, often charming and witty, and as consistently honest as they could be, considering their rather too obvious intent of pleasing rather too many people.

To my mind they are also a little sad, for their author is no free spirit despite his spectacular renunciation of public office. He professes to "draw comfort" from his marriage; at the same time he laments what that marriage entailed—"the sacrifice of my cherished British heritage along with all the years in its service." This balance of profit and loss he calls his "fate," describing himself as a "fatalist" by conviction. But surely it is a peculiar kind of fatalist who continues to argue with his fate as the Duke does here; and one recalls the cruelly perspicacious poem D. H. Lawrence wrote about him in the years when, as Prince of Wales, he was busily touring the empire and attending barbaric native ceremonies in his honor. What would the jungle men and the elephants think, Lawrence asked, "if they knew that his motto was *Ich dien?* And that he meant it."

Ich dien means "I serve," and the author of *A King's Story* still serves—serves his memories of past misfortunes, his hopes of future vindication. In no sense a fairy story, his book in a political sense is not a "story" at all but an unremitting defense of his life and work, indirectly an appeal for justice from the British people, perhaps a plea for reinstatement in some capacity among them. The Duke points to his long years of hard work as Prince of Wales; he makes clear how constraining is the monarch's position in a constitutional democracy. He argues that in abdicating he acceded, not necessarily to the wishes of the people but merely to the demands of the Baldwin circle.

Such is the Duke's defense, and to this reviewer it is not very convincing. Whether as morganatic wife or as queen, Mrs. Simpson would obviously have represented an absurd challenge to protocol and tradition, an affront to the dominions, the risk of annexing the monarchy to café society. And what would the situation be today if, besides having to acknowledge American supremacy in arms and money, Britons had also to live with the thought of an American woman in Buckingham Palace or in some adjacent hideaway? Better the Waldorf Towers! Better for the monarchy and the British people. Better for the Duke himself, if one may be so graceless as to tell a man his interests and interpret his story in a fashion contrary to his designs.

For although the Duke is ostensibly respectful toward the monarchy, he actually makes out a pretty bad case for it considered as something for a man to live with, especially a man of the Duke's English generation, for which a split notoriously developed between the claims of the public life and the claims of the private life. "Politics is the profession of the second-rate," Charles Whibley once wrote: Lytton Strachey resolved ancestral heroes into their idiosyncrasies as men and women; and only the other day E. M. Forster—an unregenerate survivor of that age—remarked that "greatness is a nineteenth-century perquisite." Clearly the Duke was once under the same spell as these typical English writers of his time. It is here that his "story" comes in and that it is seen to have the dignity of vivid truth, the fascination of being representative. For all the unique eminence of its hero, its theme is the now familiar one of spiritual dispossession. By writing his memoirs the Duke has realized his old aim of becoming one of us.

The Duke's father, George V, was a conscientious king, an exacting parent, and a profoundly simple man. He combined the monarchic with the domestic virtues to everyone's satisfaction; and he thus made very much his own position that is at once supremely magnificent in name and utterly powerless in fact. At worst there was, from the son's viewpoint, a failure of warmth on the father's part, a necessary sacrifice of family feeling to the observance of court routine and the ritual slaughter of animals in the hunt (Edward was to prefer golfing and riding to hunting). Upon this situation, not especially threatening in itself, alleviated for the Prince by his mother's unfailing tenderness, burst the war of 1914 with its terrible consequences for the stability of English society, for the youth of Edward's generation, for monarchism throughout Europe, for the prestige of authority everywhere. Edward yearned to share the dangers of war with his contemporaries but was obliged to observe them from a fairly safe distance. His sense of guilt on this score was unreasonable—no one seems to have expected him to fight—but it was nevertheless acute, and it made him tend to blame the whole monarchical system.

In the years that followed he could at least make up for his deficiencies, partly by sharing the frank pleasures and

new freedoms of what was left of his generation, partly by
pursuing conscientiously his prince's career. Now, in retro-
spect, he concedes scarcely more than Lawrence did to the
amiable legend of him as the wild prince of the twenties. Instead, he recalls mainly his princely ordeals. The din of interminable parades and speeches still sounds on his page.
One feels the horror entailed in the daily exposure of himself
to vast crowds in which the mania to touch his person was
intense and the risk of panic and death, including his own
death, was always imminent. One experiences the vanity and
folly of local officials, the oppressive smugness of Stanley
Baldwin who, though invariably "correct," seems to have
been intent on imposing himself, whether by treating his
prince to long monologues or by obliging him to listen to the
endless cracking of the ministerial fingers. Among the portraits of his former "subjects," as distinguished from those of
his family, that of Baldwin is the most elaborate in the
Duke's memoirs, where it has the symbolic purpose of showing that the king is himself a subject. Evidently Edward
could not say, like his great-grandmother, "We are not
amused."

Whether as prince or king, he is the captive of his position.
The monarchy is a symbol of the past glories of absolutism; it
can also act as a reminder of the fact that absolutism was
vanquished by the people. So long as he accepts his present
state, the royal personage is like a god; once he oversteps,
"mixes in politics" even to the extent of saying "something
must be done" to a group of unemployed miners, he is like
Bajazeth in the cage provided for him by the conquering
Tamburlane.

The Duke's response to this situation appears in the little
things he remembers as well as in the general outlines of his

career. Images of oppression and disintegration are congenial to his mind. He recalls the suffocating smell of mothballs in the robes of state, the distress of the musicians shut up in an airless hole at Windsor Castle, the jeweled cross that got dislodged from the royal crown and fell to the street during his father's funeral procession. Where the rest of us dream of glory, Edward dreamed of the commonplace. He dwells happily on those remembered moments when he or others—for he is constantly aware of others—asserted themselves against the royal routines, possessed themselves of something, however trivial. He remembers the time when his grandmother, Queen Alexandra, escaped her retinue and motored to Sandringham alone. He remembers how Henry Hansell, the tutor of the royal children, used to withdraw briefly every morning and stand alone on a low hill in the Sandringham grounds. For all its precious porcelains and Leonardo drawings, what he recalls most pleasantly about the Windsor Castle of his childhood is the launch which his parents acquired, like any bourgeois family of those years, and in which they went for excursions on the Thames. His father he pictures as sitting, at the point of death, wrapped in an old worn dressing-gown that someone had given him. His mother—who is here not at all the formidable Queen Mary of legend—is exclusively associated with the intimate and the domestic, now presiding in the nursery at the bedtime hour, now taking inventory of the family properties at Windsor.

In the thirties, as the empire tours fall off, the Prince takes to remodeling for himself a half-abandoned residence ("The Fort") on the Windsor grounds—like so many others in those years, he "fixes up an old house" in token of a desire to settle down. And presently there is Mrs. Simpson, whom he appreciates for "her American charm and energy" and because, like a Henry James heroine, she talks back to him. Ironically, he begins by admiring the gay cultivated life she shares with Simpson in their London flat, where the company, the conversation, and the cooking are of the best. And in possessing himself of her, does he not make the act doubly meaningful by taking her from another? Finally the abdication and the famous radio address. He is able at last to speak as an individual and in his own affectingly simple idiom, the idiom—almost—of the nursery; and he reprints the speech entire in his memoirs, noting that, save for two interpolations suggested by Churchill, it was entirely his work. "And now we all have a new King!"

The Duke's account of the abdication crisis is likely to become classic in the literature of memoirs. No master plotter among novelists, not even Henry James, could have invented a richer "situation" than the one that develops at this point. There is enmity without and treachery within; good motives are, however, abundant on all sides; everyone is tested to the full; and the action never flags, for no sooner has Edward decided to abdicate than a King's party materializes, led by Churchill and Beaverbrook in an adventuristic mood, and he is tempted to resist. Meanwhile Mrs. Simpson is, throughout the story, not actually divorced but only in the process of divorce; if she wished it herself or should be persuaded to it by others, she could at any moment halt the divorce proceedings and so relieve the crisis, at least momentarily. Finally, on the part of the protagonist, there is the compulsive innocence without which the plot would have been impossible in the first place. "I wish," Mrs. Simpson said to the King toward the end, "that I had had a clearer understanding of the constitutional questions." "I must take the blame for that," the King replied, "I thought it could be managed."

Only in the aftermath of the story does one feel a lack of the inevitability proper to good fiction. As one reads between the lines, takes note of the mild agonies of self-justification, feels the nostalgia for England and "The Fort," guesses how much England's grandeurs and miseries during the Blitz must have added to its stature in the Duke's eyes (as in everyone else's), one cannot but see that another ending was possible. This was a renunciation in reverse of the one actually effected by Edward: a forfeiture of private happiness, a sacrifice by which he might have secured his personal hold on the throne, made it "emotionally" his own, and then confirmed the transaction in the course of the common sufferings of himself and his subjects in wartime. But to point this out is worse than graceless, it is unrealistic; for the hero of *A King's Story* is no Henry James hero after all and his story is not a novel. It is an instance, perhaps, of what James used to call "life at its stupid work," and as such it is not without pathos and beauty.

1951

The
King
of the
Cats

For a man who lived a long time and was very active and ambitious, Yeats was unusually fortunate in his friends. Those in whom he was not so fortunate, who became his enemies, he mostly managed to outlive. "I did hate leaving the last word to George Moore," he wrote in a letter of 1927. And now after his own death he continues to be lucky in the same way. The editor of this monumental collection of Yeats's letters (*The Letters of W. B. Yeats,* edited by Allan Wade) was a member of the poet's London circle, an actor and a director of plays. He is also something that few such survivors of old times and intimates of great men ever are, a scholar. With patient labor he has assembled letters enough to fill some nine hundred pages. He has deciphered Yeats's wretched handwriting when that has been necessary, has figured out approximate dates where dates are missing, has written a commentary summarizing the events of Yeats's life from period to period, and—best of all—has identified the many obscure or semi-obscure persons addressed or alluded to in the letters. Who was Althea Gyles, of whom Yeats reports that "she brought a prosperous love-affair to an end by reading Browning to the poor man in the middle of the night"? Mr. Wade will tell you, and with just the right amount of detail.

To be sure, the volume is not as complete as its title and its huge bulk make you think it is. For one reason or another, Yeats's correspondence with several people of capital importance in his life—his wife, Maud Gonne, John Synge, Ezra Pound, Gordon Craig—had to be left out of the collection or be feebly represented in it. It is still a collection of great fascination and importance. Although some of the best things Yeats said in his letters have been used in the books about him published by Joseph Hone, Richard Ellmann and others having access to his papers, those things often sound still better in context. And of course it is context of the general as well as the specific kind that this volume supplies so plentifully. More than half a century of the poet's life is here in his own words, and with it much of the life of poetry itself from William Morris to W. H. Auden. If the ways of praising Yeats have grown dull with use and so have almost ceased to seem actively true, this book should help to renew them.

In themselves, however, his letters are not especially exhilarating. A few of them are that, in particular the later ones; and he is livelier with some of his correspondents than with others. Despite the good criticism they contain, the long series addressed to Katharine Tynan fails to reveal any adequate personal reason for its existence. Yeats seems to have thought she had the makings of a good Irish poet, but this was not enough; the letters become tedious with his effort to keep it up and not be patronizing. Even the letters to his father show the strain, and his father once complained that his son lacked "love" and made him feel like "a black beetle." (But the delightful J. B. Yeats *was* always a bit of a nag with his son.) With Olivia Shakespeare, on the other hand, Yeats is consistently engaging; she seems to have had no part in any of his projects but was simply a charming woman with whom he had once been briefly in love. For the most part, then, he had not the gift of writing letters as if he were a man living among men and women. If he has more of this feeling than, say, Wordsworth shows in his letters, he has less than, say, Byron or Keats show in theirs. Yeats's correspondents are mainly artists of some kind and are addressed by him as such. They are frankly his associates in what sometimes looks like a widespread conspiracy to be great, rather than simply to be. But he was ambitious for them as well as himself; and it is to the advantage of his letters, not to mention his poetry, that his ambition was that of the tortoise. He was a slow, patient, moral conspirator, seeking a triumph of merit. He may have said to his sister, when she told him Swinburne was dead, "I know, and now I am king of the cats," but he was no usurper. He aimed at what might be called legitimate succession, by way of a profound absorption in English poetry and a profound transformation of it. The size of his ambition, together with the conscientiousness of his methods, makes his letters extremely weighty and interesting in the mass. He was a meticulous correspondent, giving in abundance what he *could* give: ideas, plans, criticism, encouragement, anecdotes. He had a zest for the solving of problems, the meeting of situations,—a zest that his letters communicate to us. His ever-present tact did not prevent him from being quite firm, as in a long masterly letter to Sean O'Casey rejecting *The Silver Tassie* for the Abbey Theatre. His decision was probably wrong, but his reasons were compelling. The excellence with which he argues them is itself a testimonial to the importance of the occasion and the eminence of the rejected playwright. Conscious as he shows himself to be of the Irish temper—of George Moore's "incredible violence" and the "sour and argumentative" way of

Irishmen in England—he clearly cultivates amenity in his
relations with people. "It's a poet's business to be amiable,"
he tells his publisher, A. H. Bullen. But this is not the same
thing as being merely respectable: Yeats would not have relished the literary atmosphere of our bland 1950's.

Yeats was fortunate and he knew it and the knowledge colors all his letters. He seems alternately a true example of the
happy warrior in literature and a case of clinical euphoria.
He is constantly recounting his successes—with the poems or
plays he is writing, the reviewers who review his books, the
audiences who attend his plays or lectures, the famous
people he meets at parties. And his satisfaction in the material arrangements of his life makes him purr like a cat. He
rejoices in the comforts introduced into his lodgings by Lady
Gregory: the port wine and the blankets. He rejoices in his
periods of residence at Coole Park, her country house; the
"great rooms" (in the plural) are splendidly silent and there
are no fewer than seven woodlands, all magnificent. In all
this there is something of the eternal spirit of the bachelor:
he must make his nest all the cozier, and chirp the louder
over it, because it is a nest for one. The spirit persists after
Yeats's belated marriage, when he begins to celebrate his
wife's feats of housekeeping and decorating, and the attractions of the houses that he himself is now in a position to
acquire. But it must be noted that he does not long remain in
the old tower that he calls "my castle," or the house in Dublin that he describes as a "mansion." He never really settles
down; and of the money that comes to him in prizes and from
lecturing in America, he gives much to other poets and to his
various causes. In his letters he has an odd way of keeping
the phenomena of his suffering in the background. From an
allusion here and there, we may guess at the "ignominy of

boyhood" as he knew it, the hand-to-mouth existence he led in youth with his loving improvident father, his detestation of London in those days, the hardship of his life in ill-heated and candle-lighted rooms, the pain caused by his bad eyesight and frequent failures of health, the unhappy consequences of his long vain wooing of Maud Gonne, the labor of supporting himself by his writing and lecturing, the sheer fatigue of being a great poet in the twentieth century. But such experiences merely give a tragic accent to the strange high comedy of his career. Even when, in the late twenties, he breaks down and becomes very ill, he has a way of exulting in the misfortune. "Yesterday the doctor gave me a shock. I said, 'Why am I so exhausted?' He replied, 'The overwork of years.' "

Complacency or courage? A little of the first, a great deal more of the last. Yeats writes as one who has earned his good fortune, made himself lucky. "They went forth to battle but they always fell"—Matthew Arnold's motto for the Irish spirit must have rung in his ears, as it did in Joyce's, not as a knell but as a challenge. The waste of Irish genius in indolence and backbiting, the waste of his father's genius in particular, seem to have determined him to husband his own. He developed a system of thought, a method of style, an entire economy of literary action. Primarily his thought reached inward, to the power resident in the self. "Even things seemingly beyond control answer strangely to what is within," he told Florence Farr. This was applied spiritualism, table-tapping become a way of life, magic raised to the proportions of an ethic. Among the scrappy dreamers and "penitent frivolous" whom he describes as haunting Madame Blavatsky and the Golden Dawn group, he alone was to achieve, in his way, the transmutation of metals and the elixir of life.

But to his faith in the single soul was added an apprecia-
tion of the part of outward action. He had a conception of
the poet's role in the world. What this was he suggests to
John Quinn: "Keats's lines telling how Homer left great
verses to a little clan seem[ed] to my imagination when I
was a boy a description of the happiest fate that could come
to a poet." This appears always to have remained his idea of
the happy fate, and no doubt it was one he shared with
Keats, Goethe, Whitman and others who have sought ideal
audiences within the heterogeneous populations of modern
nations. For Yeats the conviction that he had a little clan was
some time in materializing. He might help to organize the
Rhymers Club in the nineties but that was not it; and the
absence in him of any strong sense of an audience helps to
account for the tremulous vagueness of his early verse. In
proportion as he acquired that sense, felt around him the
"hearers and hearteners" of his work, he developed the *viva
voce* quality, the manipulation of tone, the effect of address
or posture, which animate his mature work. But just as he had
to learn to write the "great verses," so he had to recruit the
little clan to go with them. Actually there were many clans,
ranging from his fellow occultists of the Golden Dawn to the
audiences of the Abbey Theatre; and when he had despaired
of tangible audiences he sought their Platonic counterpart in
some ideal Byzantium of the past or simply among the self-
delighting people of whatever time or place. He carried his
dream into his cosmopolitan old age, determined to the last
that he should know his audience, should feel it to be made
up of men and women like himself. "It is time that I wrote
my will: I choose upstanding men," he wrote in the great
concluding passage of "The Tower." It is hard to think of
another modern poet who would venture to cast his supreme

thought in this testamentary form, or who, having ventured it, could carry it off with Yeats's poise.

His was a poise born of conviction and based on effort. If anyone is left in the world who supposes that Yeats practiced in his life only the "wasteful virtues" he sometimes praised in his poetry, these letters will undeceive him. They show how firmly he occupied that twilight realm between dreaming and doing which he celebrated in all his poetry—the realm where anything is possible. In the end he was really the king of the cats: the greatest *lyric* poet in the language.

1956

Monstrous Dust

The recipient of these letters (*Letters to Milena* by Franz Kafka, edited by Willy Haas, translated by Tania and James Stern) was Milena Jesenká, the "M" of Kafka's later diaries. With her he corresponded at length in the early stages of a love affair that began in 1920 and lasted for some two years. He was very ill with consumption at the time; and after his death, in 1924, Milena preserved his letters, entrusting them to Willy Haas on the eve of the German invasion of Czechoslovakia. Her part in the correspondence has not survived and she herself died in a Nazi concentration camp. Mr. Haas, who tells her story in the introduction to this volume, knew her well as he had also known Kafka. He seems to have planned the book as a memorial to her.

She belonged, he writes, to a notable burgher family of Prague; and though Kafka was a native of the same city, he does not appear to have been acquainted with her there. Milena was of a younger generation and had been caught up "in the erotic and intellectual promiscuity of the Viennese literary café society in the wild years after 1918." Even in that setting she was a rarity: "passionate, intrepid," "a character such as Stendhal lifted out of the old Italian chronicles." When Kafka first knew her, Milena was twenty-four and lived in Vienna with a husband from whom she thought of separating. She taught school, wrote for the magazines, admired Stevenson as well as Dostoevsky, and had been quick to see the genius of Kafka's few published stories. She had undertaken to translate his *Metamorphosis* into Czech, and it was while corresponding about this project that they discovered one another.

To reconstruct the affair in its external developments would be tedious if not impossible in the present state of the letters, which the editor admits to be quite unsettled. Mostly undated, often unclear in their allusions to events and people, supplied with a minimum of editorial notes, and occasionally deleted "out of consideration for persons still alive," the letters must be read as a mere monologue. It hardly matters. So far as one can make out, "our relationship," as Kafka (or the translators) drearily term it, was probably uneventful. Kafka and Milena rarely met; and as Mr. Haas remarks, "their love was essentially a letter-love, like the love of Kierkegaard or Werther."

Not quite. Kafka was more enterprising than Kierkegaard, not to mention Werther. When he and Milena did meet, it was almost certainly to go to bed. Neither his diaries nor the present letters make any secret of his fierce intermittent sensuality. In this, he tells Milena, he had something in him of "the eternal Jew, wandering senselessly through a senselessly obscene world." It was the urge of the dispossessed for possession of the promised land, of the estranged for reunion with mankind. And although the affair with Milena looked hopeless from the start, neither of them abandoned it without a moral struggle as fierce as the sensuality. At first Kafka is tempted to continue it: he is eager for some permanent union. But before long he is writing, "we never can or will live together." His reasons are many: he is a Jew and she is not; he is too old, too sick; and anyway she is only "dazzled" by his writings. Conceivably, his very passion for her is generated by his mortal illness and despair. If he "belongs to her," it is by virtue of "this whole monstrous dust which 38 years have kicked up and which has settled in my lungs." She on her side combats and derides his scruples but cannot prevail against the monstrous dust, which is his accumulated experience of tragedy. She must remain his "angel of death."

They had, besides, a number of lesser misunderstandings. They brought into the affair too many of their friends. Kafka induces Milena to correspond with Max Brod: they fail to hit it off. Milena asks Kafka to hunt up in Prague an old acquaintance of hers named Jarmila: the issue is doubtful. Some acrimony is created by a mysterious mission that Milena has urged him to undertake and that she thinks he has bungled. Meanwhile there is Ernest, Milena's husband, toward whom Kafka is oddly propitiatory, not only because Ernest is a rival but because he is that—to Kafka—enviable thing, a Husband. Finally there is "the girl," Kafka's fiancée of several months (the "J.W." of the diaries), whom he is trying to break with: the girl also writes to Milena. Thinking of Milena, her husband and himself, Kafka describes the situation as *"torture à trois,"* but he seems to have miscounted.

And indeed love, their love, is constantly depicted by Kafka as a disastrous experience. For Milena it will mean "to leap into an abyss"; for him she is "the knife which I turn within myself." Kafka's ambivalent feeling toward love and marriage is well known. It had, at this point, brought him failure in three major campaigns (the one engagement to "J.W.," the two separate engagements to "F.B."); and he was becoming intensely conscious of himself as a veteran with many wounds and no trophies. "Sisyphus was a bachelor," he noted

in his diaries during those years. In the case of Milena, however, one suspects that special irritants were at work and that
her being young, romantic, gentile, impelled him to a peculiar vehemence. He wants, perhaps, to divest her of her illu-
sions about life. So she is spared nothing of his situation—
past, present and to come. His oppressive father, his cruel
childhood, his "obscene" sexual history, his mortal thinness
of body, his insomnia, his coughing fits, his dreams—all are
made to contribute to her enlightenment. Increasingly, he
reminds her of his Jewishness. "This means, expressed with
exaggeration, that not one calm second is granted me, nothing is granted me, everything has to be earned." "My nature
is: Fear." At one moment Prague is full of Jewish refugees
from revolutionary Russia and there are anti-Semitic riots in
the streets. He spends an entire afternoon among the demon-
strators, "wallowing" in the spectacle. On this occasion his
cries are dreadful to overhear, like those of a man in the embrace of a nightmare. As Mr. Haas observes, for Kafka the
"love of a non-Jew was evidently a serious, tragic problem."

Yes, but all of life tended to become such a problem for
him. The inescapable unity of his experience was his despair,
his joke and his glory. His candor in expressing, in *feeling*,
his situation as a Jew was like a fire in which that situation
got refined of all local, temporal, special considerations and
so came to serve his great primary art. "Out of the quarrel
with ourselves, we make poetry," in Yeats's phrase. Elsewhere in the letters, at calmer moments, he writes about his
people in a spirit which has little to do with Milena, much to
do with his mind and art. "The insecure position of Jews,
insecure within themselves, insecure among people, would
make it above all comprehensible that they consider themselves to be allowed to own only what they hold in their

hands or between their teeth, that furthermore only palpable possessions give them the right to live, and that they will never regain what they once have lost but that instead it calmly swims away from them forever." A similar paradox gives energy to Kafka's fiction, in which man in general is shown as holding life "between his teeth" in return for the insecurity of his spiritual existence. And this conception, which distinguishes Kafka from Kierkegaard no less than from Eliot (for whom religion is so much a matter of "belief," and unbelief is so often associated with mere debility), Kafka owes to the tradition of Moses, Job and Ruth. His unique place among the great recent writers consists in his bringing that tradition to bear on the preoccupations of modernity.

There are in the *Letters to Milena* other evidences of the Kafka who had written *The Trial* and was soon to write *The Castle*. These, however, are mostly evidences of his general mind and style, rarely of his opinions or his reading. For all his distress, he usually sustains a good-humored composure: certainly it is often humorous, a kind of intricate teasing. Here as in his stories he keeps to the imponderable line between horror and farce, the physical and the spiritual, the intensely personal and the brilliantly impersonal. Even his macabre jokes at the expense of the Jews recall Swift's "A Modest Proposal," which he knew. For the rest, one constantly surprises his genius for invention at its characteristic work. Milena's husband, whom he used to see in the Prague cafés, had "the peculiarity of being called to the telephone several times during the evening. Presumably there must have been someone who, instead of sleeping, sat by the telephone dozing, his head on the back of his chair, and who sat up from time to time to call him." The letters abound in anecdote, parable, paradox (a little too much of this last). The entire experience with Milena is thus translated into Kafka's animated moral idiom—as he says, "rearranged for my orchestra." (The effects are probably much attenuated in English although the translation sounds convincing.)

But it would be to take an intolerably high line with these letters to assert that the humor and eloquence erase the impression of suffering. The impression of suffering is indelible; and to our present age, with its cult of the reconstructed ego and the busy life, Kafka's letters will come as intrusive reminders of the lost art of being unhappy. This art, which one may call the art of introspection, gives Kafka his peculiar authority in suffering. It permits him to see his own life in its entirety and to connect it, by way of observation and myth, with the life of everyone. It is with more than authority, with pride, that he says to Milena: "I believe I understand the Fall of Man as no one else."

1954

The
Romance
of Charles
Chaplin

One of the many fine things about Chaplin's *My Autobiography* is that it includes, along with an exhaustive index and
a lot of photographs, a "List of the Films of Charles Chaplin." Thus we learn that his first movie—or if he insists, film
—dates from 1914 and was entitled *Making a Living*. In all
senses of the word "living," Chaplin has since made it. No
other movie career, and few recent literary careers, have
yielded so much continuous delight over so many years as
his has. It has also included a period of what might be called
"total crisis," one of those situations in which the hero of a
mass society undergoes a bitter reversal of fortune, public
and private, and becomes for a time a prominent scapegoat.
In Chaplin's case, this deplorable turn has not proved ruin-
ous. On the contrary, his present life as described in *My
Autobiography* resembles the last act of a late-Shakespearean
romance. Order has been restored, love is requited, paternity
is triumphant, and there has been a general reunion with the
universe—possibly excepting the United States. In this country, however, many of his films are again on view; and while
you endure that "short wait in the lobby for seats," you are
gratified to hear issuing from the auditorium gusts of unembarrassed, in fact uncontrollable, laughter. Even "the children," whom you have taken along, with some fear as to

their possible reactions, soon get into the spirit and join the great collectivity of Chaplin-inspired mirth and adoration. A student did once tell the present writer that Chaplin's comic style lacked "moral reference" and was a little dated. It is the unfortunate student who seems a little dated now— if such things matter.

Charles Chaplin would therefore appear to be the perfect subject for an autobiography. Yet it has been reported that he was at first a reluctant subject and only yielded to his publishers' persuasion after much debate. No doubt the report is true. It was not in him to turn out an unconsidered performance inevitably labeled *The Charlie Chaplin Story*. And apart from the sheer labor of doing a thorough job, he may have felt some doubt about his competence to do it. True, he has shown a distinct largeness of ambition in those films where he was actor, director, script writer, and composer. But he has given no sign of thinking himself an accomplished man of letters with a command of literary form and style, and with the more or less settled convictions about life and art that are implied in those things. He commands them in his own elusive medium but the verbal medium is patently something else. Besides, the "person" behind Chaplin's work has always seemed a little inaccessible. And while these problems may or may not have figured in his deliberations before he decided to write his autobiography, they do figure for the reader of the completed work.

There are of course two Chaplins, Charles Chaplin and Charlie. The pair as such are well known in Chaplin lore; and their existence argues no large or lurid complexity on either's part, no war of rival identities between them. It is only a working partnership. The two get along so well together because they are so unlike. One of them is out of this world while the other is very much of it. Charlie the clown is an extreme case of artfully blended antitheses. He is a dandified tramp, a Pierrot of the industrial age, an ideally resourceful male with an ideal female's winning grace and solicitous sweetness. Charlie is a dream—but a dream that much solid stuff is made of. In the way he twitches a property mustache or slices with a knife a derby hat doused in a creamy sauce, believing the hat to be a real pudding, there is a multitude of all too human suggestions. Twitched mustaches are implausible by nature. All dinner party embarrassments approximate to the impact of cold steel on creamed felt, setting the teeth on edge.

Like a dream, too, Charlie is more eloquent for being silent. "The matrix out of which he was born was as mute as the rags he wore," Charles Chaplin remarks in the autobiography. By "matrix" he means, it will be seen, several things. In one of its senses, it is another word for the visual imagination, which Chaplin exploited and glorified in his pre-talkie films. At first he hated the sound track with its elaborate apparatus and specialized personnel. Charlie's essential being was threatened by electronic sound. It was an intruder upon the house of the visual imagination, a thief in the silence of Charlie's enchanted night. Charles Chaplin's job was to come to Charlie's assistance and rout the intruder, at least for a while. His role in the partnership was always to serve Charlie as guardian and general utility man. Charles took Charlie's measure when the future looked alarming. He foresaw that his alter ego's possibilities were relative to his alter ego's limitations, that his survival depended on his remaining what he had always been: an extreme case of refined artifice. No real concessions were to be made to new film technologies and styles of laughter. Thus Charlie was enabled to outlast many a less specialized, but also less conscious, artist who, through the competitive processes of comedy, was quickly to become a has-been or a hack or, like Walt Disney, an industry. When Charlie's time finally came he was put away, and his silence silenced, by a reluctant but realistic Charles.

Did a merger of the two take place after that, in the period of *Monsieur Verdoux* and *Limelight?* Or did Charlie Chaplin take over the whole firm? The question is silly. Half truths about dual identities can be manipulated to the point of becoming schematic. Yet in *My Autobiography* the author himself makes some random use of the Charles-Charlie duality, evidently with the purpose of enlivening the narrative and keeping its sprawling bulk in perspective.

The book does sprawl. It is a very strenuous exercise in total recall. Chaplin might have fixed upon a single representative moment or situation in his life, for example the making of *City Lights,* with all the important decisions, the professional problems, and the personalities that were involved in it. Instead he chose to attempt the usual full-blown survey and to present it in the usual chronological form. But is Chaplin's life, in its really significant aspects, conventional or usual? One's reading of the autobiography suggests the contrary. The career that was his essential glory seems much farther removed from the rest of his experience than would normally be the case if the autobiographer were a statesman or a writer or, for that matter, a different kind of actor. Given his beautifully specialized art, Chaplin's experiences as celebrity, lover, husband, and political prophet are of questionable relevance. At best they belong to the social history of movies. Yet he shows little talent or inclination for treating this subject. The people he portrays tend to remain indistinct; the conversations he reports, often in dialogue form, sound vaguely fabricated. It is as if everybody were on stilts, even jolly Douglas Fairbanks, Chaplin's most congenial friend. As a writer he can't work up enough feeling, either sympathetic or malicious, to make his associates—friends or non-friends—interesting. As a result, his own personality goes dim—becomes, as I say, inaccessible—for long stretches. He seems to be conducting a rather formal interview with himself. "What do I think of Mr. Churchill?" "I think Mr. Churchill is . . ." What is lacking is not candor; on the subject of people, as well as on his political and moral beliefs, he is generally forthright. An unrepentant exile from the United States, he is quite unafraid of giving offense to that ignorant and vindictive element of the American public that once found him *persona non grata. My Autobiography* is the work of a man who, in his own eyes, is not "controversial" but historic. His candor, however, is a quality of his moral intelligence alone. As an observer of persons and manners, Chaplin gets little help from it.

His adventures in Celebrityland are nevertheless told at length: those obligatory encounters with predictable personages from Shaw to Gandhi, Lady Astor to Elinor Glyn. Is anybody absent? Yes, Albert Schweitzer. But then, Albert Einstein is present. And Churchill, although he is everybody's star-celebrity, gets more space in the book than *Modern Times,* a unique masterpiece.

Is Chaplin aware of the irrelevance of it all? Probably. In the chapters concerning his travels and triumphs, Charlie the clown is, as I said, revived. He is invested with the skeptic's viewpoint and assigned the role of victim in the celebrity game. The procedure is too consistent to have been accidental; and the author's intentions, as I understand them, are of the best. He hopes to restore the balance by keeping his great comic counterpart in the picture. So the narrative is strewn with memories of small embarrassments suffered by himself and others in the Vanity Fair of world fame. Most of these incidents involve bits of brisk and punishing "business." In short they are "slapstick" and recall the comic routines in his movies. For example his contretemps with William Randolph Hearst. Once during luncheon at San Simeon the two of them disagree about a projected movie venture. Hearst becomes quite irritated. "When I say a thing is white you always say it is black," he tells Chaplin, who, feeling insulted, calls for a taxi and leaves the table. But he is quickly overtaken in another room by a remorseful Hearst who sits Chaplin down beside him in a small double seat of the Chippendale period and proceeds to make peace. Peace being made, the two then start to get up to return to the dining room. But they discover they are stuck in the valuable antique. With the insane splendors of San Simeon as background, this tale has a point.

A better story, with a more extended gag, has to do with Chaplin and Jean Cocteau. Indirectly, perhaps, it is also a comment on the strange logic of existence in Celebrityland, of which both men were of course ranking citizens and knew it. The two meet for the first time by chance on shipboard during a China Sea crossing. Cocteau expresses his joy that the long delayed meeting has finally taken place. They spend a night in rapturous conversation, although neither is well acquainted with the other's language and Cocteau's secretary makes an indifferent interpreter. They part towards dawn with enthusiastic assurances of future talks. But a couple of mornings later, when the two are about to collide on deck, Cocteau suddenly ducks into the ship's interior. And throughout the rest of the interminable day ahead, their relations will consist in a series of artful dodgings and hearty but decisive hails and farewells. It appears that a mysterious magnetic force is at work in Celebrityland to guarantee that any two of its ranking citizens will inevitably meet—somewhere, somehow. With Chaplin and Cocteau, the mysterious force seems to have got out of hand, like the feeding machine in *Modern Times*. Their off and on friendship also recalls that of the Tramp and the alcoholic millionaire in *City Lights*, made several years before Chaplin met Cocteau.

Charlie's interventions brighten a little the social picture in *My Autobiography*. And presently the picture changes. The social scene is more or less taken over by "Salka Viertel, the Clifford Odetses, the Hanns Eislers, the Feuchtwangers," and Thomas Mann and Bertolt Brecht. These friends reflected, possibly stimulated, Chaplin's increasingly explicit concern with what he calls "the fate of the world," a concern that was already apparent in the explicit satire of *Modern Times* (1936). For the world as for him the total crisis was at hand. Along with the Nazi horrors, the war, and Soviet Russia's entrance into it, there was the question of the Second Front. No doubt the arrival of the illustrious refugees in his vicinity brought home to him the human reality of the general terror. Chaplin's personal and professional life was similarly beset by difficulties. His labors on *Monsieur Verdoux*, a radically new venture, coincided with his forced participation in the grotesque "paternity suit." In eyes bleared by the prevailing hysteria, he stood convicted of moral turpitude and political unreliability, always a sinister compound. An impertinent reporter remarked to him during an interview: "Your public relations are not very good."

They were not, and his account of the crisis in his autobiography is unlikely to improve them. Not that his public relations are the affair, or the real concern, of a sympathetic reviewer. What must be said, however, is that he shows no inclination to reconsider his own political attitudes of the time, in the interests either of mere appeasement (God forbid) or of historical truth and autobiographical self-discovery. He emerges from the crisis in the role of pure victim—a role that is too exciting to be quite believable. With such an embattled figure argument is fruitless, and where Chaplin is concerned there are better things to do than argue politics. As Robert Warshow, Chaplin's best critic, wrote: "The impact of his art . . . was helped rather than hindered by a certain simplicity in his conceptions of political and social problems." "Conceptions?" A better word might be "dreams."

My Autobiography is more convincing about family history and about the history of the movies as reflected in Chaplin's own work. One learns that he began asserting his authority as a film maker rather earlier than one had thought. During his very first year (1914) in movies, while he was still with the Keystone Company, Mack Sennett suddenly set Mabel Normand to directing Chaplin's pictures. She was a nice girl and pretty but "incompetent." He objected, pacified Mabel, and became a part-time director himself. To be sure, as he says, improvisation was rampant in the studios in those days. He loved it. After touring for years in uninspired stage plays he had, one guesses, stored up a wealth of unused inventiveness. It spilled out under the benign anarchy at Keystone. In time he seemed to us, his public, to inhabit a realm where sheer inventiveness was the rule. Hence the peculiar exhilaration his films imparted to his audiences, and the bonus of personal affection his audiences gave him in return.

They understood what his "moral reference" consisted in. He made them feel agile, creative, free, happy. There was even something chancy about the origins of the Tramp's costume, inevitable as it seems now. Mack Sennett merely told him one day: "We need some gags here. Put on a comedy make-up. Anything will do." So Chaplin headed for the wardrobe and grabbed some "baggy pants, big shoes, a cane and a derby hat. I wanted everything a contradiction: the pants baggy, the coat tight, the hat small and the shoes large. I was undecided whether to look old or young, but remembering Sennett had expected me to be a much older man, I added a small moustache." He had "no idea of the character" at first, but once he was in costume the character was "fully born" and "gags and comedy ideas went racing through my mind." Still, improvisation had limits. There had to be a director like Mack Sennett to make decisions, as well as to reverse them, even while, like Mack Sennett himself, he "giggled until his body began to shake" at the doings of Fatty Arbuckle, Ford Sterling, Mabel Normand, and Charlie Chaplin.

As an autobiographer, then, Chaplin is more at home on the Keystone and Essanay lots than he will later be at San Simeon, Pickfair, and the Prince of Wales's Fort Belvedere (private residences which, incidentally, he tends to describe as if they were hotels, remarking critically on the "furnishings" and the "cuisine"). But he is most at ease in the first hundred or so pages, where the subject is his early experiences as a London waif and incipient actor. Those experiences were the ultimate "matrix" out of which Chaplin and Charlie emerged.

Most autobiographers are best on such distant and "formative" years. Chaplin's childhood seems exceptionally close to him and it was formative with a vengeance. His childhood was made to order to destroy a waif or foster a genius. In its concentrated burden of extreme situations it surpassed Dickens's famous childhood. Everything was extreme: the hardness of the hardship, the sweetness of the satisfactions. Home was the more ideally homelike because one was so often homeless. A mother's devotion was the more prized because it was frequently unavailable. Did "things happen," as children are always wishing things will? Things happened without let-up. The days were not only eventful; they were a perpetual flow, or flood, of elemental event. No wonder Chaplin was to be so different from his associates, in Hollywood and elsewhere. He tells us that the cockney-born H. G. Wells worried about his (Wells's) misplaced h's. In Chaplin's case some part of *himself* was misplaced by his early deprivations and has remained forever estranged from the world, even though capable of forming that working partnership with Charles Chaplin.

His Old World past, his almost *prehistoric* past, survives in Chaplin like a vital organ. Often though his family moved from flat to flat in South London, he remembers perfectly the street numbers and the "furnishings." He can recall, it appears, just about everything, and in the early chapters of *My Autobiography* he does so with a zest that is largely absent from the remainder of the book. The misery of that time speaks for itself. The autobiographer is thus at liberty to find satisfaction in the act of recall itself, in the precise art of retracing the child's million steps up and down greasy stairs, in and out of cheerless interiors, back and forth along dingy streets. (*Easy Street?* For something that resembles the *Easy Street* set, see the photograph in the book with the legend: "Where we lived, next to the slaughterhouse and the pickle factory, after Mother came out of the asylum.") So "real" is that entire past of his, so intimately and completely *his*, that the writer is freed from self-consciousness and can take a simple delight in the story, just as he will later show delight in recalling the time his mother said "shit."

Here, it may be assumed, memory works an uncommonly complete transformation even while it seems to be engaged in a powerful attempt at faithful representation. Chaplin's memory possesses it all too firmly for distortion to occur. Yet everything indicates that in actuality, at the time, the child was conscious of possessing little that he was sure was his own and could call "real." His childhood was the scene, not of poverty and neglect alone, but of a more inclusive kind of distress. People and places and things were constantly disappearing. Some of them turned up again and again. But would they turn up the next time? Life was a perpetual vanishing act. Or wasn't it?

"In my world of three and a half years, all things were possible; if Sydney, who was four years older than I, could perform legerdemain and swallow a coin and make it come out through the back of his head, I could do the same; so I swallowed a halfpenny and Mother was obliged to send for the doctor." Coins got scarcer later on. His parents, both of them originally popular performers in music halls, were separated and his father took to drink and his mother's health failed. The boy and his father became strangers or worse: intermittent relatives. They shared a flat when his mother was ill, then met at long intervals and by chance in streets and bars. His mother and Sydney (her son by a mysterious earlier union with an English gentleman in Africa) made up the family for Charles. In health, she was loving, attentive, amusing: a rare combination of maternal and theatrical instincts. There were recitations, impersonations, burlesques in the house. But her stage voice presently gave out and her theatrical engagements dwindled. At five, Charles replaced her on stage one night when she was suddenly incapacitated, and he finally made his exit showered with coins.

The family is now close to destitution. Mrs. Chaplin takes up religion and earns sixpences doing piecework as a seamstress. Her mind begins to distintegrate; there are spells of gentle madness, brought on, the doctors say, by malnutrition. She is in and out of asylums. The boys are in and out of workhouses where flogging is still routine and Charles on one occasion gets his. Somehow he and Sydney survive. The family's theatrical tradition is the legacy that saves them. At twelve, Charles gets his first important part (in *Jim: The Romance of a Cockney*) and although scarcely literate enough to read the script, he is a hit and on his way. With an act called The Eight Lancashire Lads, he tours the provinces: the ever-changing London habitations of his childhood are replaced by endless small town hotels. Being an actor is hard and lonely work, and not only in England. In America, where he eventually arrives with the Karno Company, he is again on tour and once more it is hotels, hotels. But something has been added, an American speciality of the period: the red light districts.

His love for his mother also survived. Of all the people mentioned in *My Autobiography*, she alone is portrayed fully and freely. His feeling for her puts aside the usual barriers of his constraint. She exists, and wonderfully, remembered in all the pity, the irony, the strange fun, of her condition. Amazingly, she herself survived, to spend her final years near Los Angeles after Chaplin had become famous and was able to tell her that he was worth five million dollars. In Cali-

fornia, it appears, she still had spells of mild insanity, thus
providing material for some of the weirder gags in the *Autobiography.* Once during a visit to an ostrich farm she was
shown an ostrich egg by the keeper and, snatching it, she
cried, "Give it back to the poor bloody ostrich!" and tossed
the egg into the corral, "where it exploded with a loud report." Another time, out riding on a hot afternoon in her
chauffeur-driven car, she leaned out to hand an ice cream
cone to a workman in the street and accidentally threw it in
his face. It seems that maternal instinct, like everything else,
can go awry. Still another time she asked her son, "Wouldn't
you rather be yourself than live in this theatrical world of
unreality?" and he replied with a laugh, "You should talk."

Perhaps she wasn't so naïve. The problem of "being himself" has obviously vexed Chaplin even more than it does the
rest of us. It forms a major theme, though an unformulated
one, in *My Autobiography.* The circumstances that gave rise
to the problem are written large in his account of his childhood. Considering the phantasmagoria of impermanence he
lived in, it is a wonder the child could remember his name,
let alone his latest address. Naturally, he clung to them, as to
his mother's affection and other things, with a tenacity born
of his very desperation. Naturally, too, the Tramp would
eventually re-enact the essentials of that experience in terms
of free invention and comic artifice. Homeless, speechless,
nameless, indefinitely on the run, the Tramp finds his true
love only to lose her, and possesses himself of the girl's grace
and sweetness in lieu of possessing the girl. Nor is it unlikely,
judging by his autobiography, that the Charles-Charlie partnership was his salvation as a person and an artist, just because it was, as already indicated, a *working* partnership.
With actual women, on the other hand, his relations are

somewhat obscured by his tact: many of the women are still alive. He does say, apropos of one early affair, that "No woman could measure up to that vague image I had in my mind." Possibly he means to suggest that he was perpetually trailed by the maternal presence, or absence, at least until his present marriage. In any case he brings a peculiar gaiety to his accounts of his more casual affairs. The girls include one nameless European who, after agreeing to a short-time affair, seems to have fallen for him and become a bother, until, resigned at last to losing him, she accompanied him to his ship at Naples, waved a cheerful good-bye from the dock, and made off into the blue yonder walking the Charlie walk. Lucky girl. Lucky Charlie.

1964

It Shows
Shine: Notes
on Gertrude
Stein

There used to be something known to all readers as "Steinese." This was the peculiar literary idiom invented by Gertrude Stein around 1910 and made familiar to a large American public by her admirers and nonadmirers alike. Gnomic, repetitive, illogical, sparsely punctuated, Steinese became a scandal and a delight, lending itself equally to derisory parody and fierce denunciation. It had a formidable currency in writing and conversation throughout the teens, twenties, and thirties. "A rose is a rose is a rose" and "Pigeons on the grass alas" were encountered as frequently—almost— as the "Yes, we have no bananas," a nonsense phrase—later a song—of popular origin which may actually have been inspired by Steinese. "My little sentences have gotten under their skins," Gertrude Stein was at last able to say, with the pride of someone who craved recognition the more that she got mere notoriety. Her little sentences, originally quoted in scorn, had come in time to be repeated from something like affection; and thus the very theory that underlay her technique of reiteration was proved: what people loved they repeated, and what people repeated they loved.

Simple-minded though she sounded to the public, Gertrude Stein had her theories—few writers of note have had more stringent ones. If she was "the Mother Goose of Montparnasse," as someone said (such attempts to characterize her in a witty phrase were constantly repeated, too), she was a Mother Goose with a mind. She had studied psychology with William James at Radcliffe; conducted laboratory experiments there with Hugo Münsterberg; come close to getting an M.D. at Johns Hopkins; and then, settling in Paris with her brother Leo, had communed with Picasso in his Paris studio where a different kind of experiment was in progress: the plastic analysis of spatial relations which gave rise to Cubist painting.

Thus, behind the popular image, scornful or condescending, of Gertrude Stein there came to be a woman of immense purpose, equipped with astonishing powers of assimilation, concentration and hard work—as well as, to be sure, relaxation (she liked to lie in the sun and stare right into it). Her meeting with Picasso was in itself purely fortuitous; such a meeting might have befallen any tourist with a mildly questing spirit and enough money to buy paintings which, in any event, went almost begging. Gertrude Stein converted this meeting into the basis of a vocation and a life. It became for her the major case—her acquaintance with William James was a lesser case—of genius by association. Her scientific interests now fused with a passion, at last fully awakened, for art and literature. Out of this union of the laboratory and the studio came a body of theory and writing like none before or after it. True, there were elements in it of the Naturalism that was just then (ca. 1900) taking root in American literature. So far as these elements alone went, Gertrude Stein might have been a Dreiser manqué—except that, with her Cubist predilections, she became, as it were, post-Dreiser. Like Dreiser and other literary Naturalists she held quasi-scientific conceptions of race and individual character; life, moreover, expressed itself best in forms of "struggle" (the word was frequently hers as it was that of Dreiser's generation: "the class struggle," "the struggle for existence"). Her first mature work, *Three Lives,* was a triple portrait of the servant, a type of oppressed individual with a special appeal for novelists of the Naturalist tendency, from Flaubert and the Goncourt brothers to Dreiser himself; in addition, her trio, two German girls and a Negro girl, belonged to ethnic minorities, another staple Naturalist subject. Yet *Three Lives* proved to be a study in the language, syntax, and rhythms of consciousness rather than in the effects of oppression, social or cosmic. Here her aesthetic predilections checkmated and partially transformed the Dreiserian elements. *Three Lives* remains her most widely admired book.

The American writer who most attracted her was not Dreiser or any of his school but Henry James. And there may have been personal as well as aesthetic reasons for her refusal of Naturalist pessimism and protest and her liking for the less doctrinaire, the more free-spirited, realism of Henry James. Gertrude Stein felt no urgent identification with the oppressed; life was a struggle that she could very probably win. Her grandparents had been German-Jewish immigrants and they had prospered in the United States; her parents, prospering too, had been beguiled by art, languages, and educational theory. As children, Gertrude Stein and her sister and brothers, like the young Jameses at an earlier period, had been transported to Europe for a prolonged stay in some of its great cities. Thus the impression left by the elder Steins, at least on Gertrude Stein, was that of people who had to a considerable degree done as they liked and made themselves at home equally in America and Europe. No doubt their example, as she conceived of it, fortified her own determination to do the same, do even better. Hence the impulse, so patiently and passionately followed by her, to root herself in a profession, in the city of Paris, in a society of her choosing.

The consequences for her personality were, again, astonishing. In her maturity, she gave the impression, not merely of doing what she liked but of *being* almost anything she wanted to be. She seemed, as the many surviving likenesses of her suggest, at once female and male, Jew and non-Jew, American *pur sang* and European peasant, artist and public figure. She did not, however, create this intricate unity and sustain it without showing evidences of great strain. Her magnetic, almost magical, self-mastery was buttressed by frank self-indulgence and advertised to the world by a good deal of unashamed self-congratulation. A regular system of compensations characterized her ideas, her tastes, her associations—everything that made up her manner of life. Inclusions entailed exclusions in a virtually mechanical perfection of balance. For almost every idea she embraced, almost every person she befriended, there was some idea that remained pointedly alien to her, some person who was an outsider. Henry James had played something like this drama too, though with more compunction, it seems, and with himself often cast as the outsider. Gertrude Stein, never the outsider, seems not to have risen—or sunk—to the level of James's flexibility. Thus her combined residence, salon, and art gallery in the rue de Fleurus, where she presided with the aid of the devoted Miss Toklas, presented the aspects, now of an infinitely charming refuge, now of a bristling fortress. It was the citadel of that new spirit of connoisseurship which, applied to all things, from the writing of a sentence to the cooking of an artichoke, made life a joy and an ordeal for

so many young Americans of the period. The charming aspect of the rue de Fleurus predominated; the wariest visitor
was apt to be struck by things about Gertrude Stein that
were more literally magical than her self-mastery—things
that were not to be fully accounted for by will, intelligence,
or the principle of genius by association: her magnificent
head and features, her appealing voice, her elementally re-
freshing laugh.

II

But Gertrude Stein's family history cannot have been the
only source, or even the principal one, of her prodigious and
largely good-humored will to power. The same background
failed to supply her brother Leo with any such determination to make himself at home in the world. Brilliant, erratic,
eternally unfulfilled, Leo Stein became an early advocate
and perennial patient of psychoanalysis, finding a sort of
fatherland only in Freud. In Gertrude Stein's case, obviously,
it was her involvement in the profession of literature, and the
exacting mysteries attending it, that made the difference.
The profession was the more engrossing because of the variety of influences she brought to bear on it. If her conception
of literature included elements of Naturalism, it also antici-
pated the literary Modernism that was to culminate in the
chief works of such writers as Joyce, Eliot, Yeats, and Pound.
To her as to them (up to a point), literature in the twentieth
century presented itself as a problem in the reconstruction of
form and language. But where the solution of this problem
was a means to an end for these writers, it became, for her,
on the whole, a pursuit worthy in itself of her best efforts.

She had no quarrel, as they did, with culture, with history, with the self. Culture in her terminology becomes "composition," a neutral aggregate of institutions, technologies, and human relations which the artist, as artist, accepts as it is, eliciting its meanings primarily through eye and ear rather than through mind, memory, or imagination. And words, like the other materials of the literary medium, become useful to the artist, assume a character purely aesthetic, in proportion as they can be converted from bearers of established meaning and unconscious association into plastic entities.

Such, very briefly, was the theoretical basis of her work, a basis to which she added many refinements as she sought to find literary equivalents for the various experiments conducted by the Cubists. Her theories have been admirably expounded and criticized in a number of recent books. The usual conclusion is the common sense one. Literature is a temporal art rather than, like painting, a spatial one; and in being used as plastic entities, as things in themselves, words become not more but less alive, indeed peculiarly inert. Mr. Kenneth Burke has called Gertrude Stein's practice "art by subtraction," a phrase that expresses well the literal and merely negative aspect of her work at its least effective. Mr. B. L. Reid has made Burke's phrase the title of a hostile study of Gertrude Stein; and Mr. John Malcolm Brinnin, in *The Third Rose*, the best biography of her, sums up his investigations into her methods as follows:

> Language is plastic, but its plasticity must be informed and determined by the philosophy or, at least, by the information it conveys. In her earlier works, Gertrude Stein operated under this injunction naturally; but as she continued, her attraction to painting led her to wish for the same plastic freedom for literature, and eventually to write as though literature

were endowed with such freedom. "The painter," said Georges
Braque, "knows things by sight; the writer, who knows them
by name, profits by a prejudice in his favor." This was the
profit Gertrude Stein threw away.

All this applies to darkest Stein. Mr. Brinnin and many
others, including the present writer, find this territory difficult of access. Nor, of course, is one helped by having
learned one's way around in, say, *Finnegans Wake* and *Four
Quartets*. On the contrary, a knowledge of Joyce's or Eliot's
methods sets one to looking in Gertrude Stein for meanings
and values according to the principle of unconscious association. But this is the wrong principle to apply to, for example,
Tender Buttons. Gertude Stein insisted that she was not
practicing "automatic writing" or working in any literary
convention, such as Surrealism, related to automatic writing.
No release of unconscious impulses, her own or those of fictional characters, is intended. She must, in fact, have devoted
much labor to eliminating such suggestions. Thus the body
of her theory and writing at its most advanced occupies
an anomalous position among the various modern schools.
Where they all begin—by asserting the primacy of the literary "medium" (words)—Gertrude Stein for the most part
begins and ends.

The usual theoretical objections to her work are persuasive; yet between them and her work itself there is always a
certain accusing margin of doubt. Poets have found her work
exciting, however inexplicably so, as if words in themselves
might in certain circumstances appeal to some receptive apparatus in man that is comparable to what people call extra-
sensory perception. This is not, on the whole, the experience
of the present writer in the farther reaches of Gertrude Stein.
Yet, read aloud, certain passages in, say, *Tender Buttons,* do

make their effect, especially if read in the company of people prepared to laugh or start or otherwise express the sudden access of the sense of wonder. The silent reader expects familiar rewards for his efforts. The *viva voce* reader is more apt to take what comes and make the most of it. To the ear, when it is lent freely to a given passage of Stein, the contrast stands out between, on the one hand, the perpetual flow of *non sequiturs* and, on the other, the air of conviction conveyed by the very definite words, the pregnant pauses, the pat summary phrases ("This is this," "It is surely cohesive," "It is not the same"); and the mingling of apparent conviction with transparent nonsense throughout such a passage takes on its own kind of momentary sense, giving rise (if the reader is lucky) to a wondering laugh. As one of her pat phrases suggests, "It shows shine." Does it also *show Stein?* If so, reading these tongue-twisting words aloud helps to bring the pun to light. So too with the occasional rhymes and jingles strewn through this prose: they also come alive better when spoken.

Tender Buttons is probably Gertrude Stein's most "private" performance. The verbal still-lifes in that book defy even Mr. Donald Sutherland, the critic who, in *Gertrude Stein: A Biography of Her Work,* has made more headway than anyone else in interpreting her prose. Here is a passage, surely very beautiful, from "Lend a Hand or Four Religions" (in *Useful Knowledge,* 1928), followed by Mr. Sutherland's comment:

> First religion. She is feeling that the grasses grow four times yearly and does she furnish a house as well. . . . Let her think of a stable man and a stable can be a place where they care for the Italians every day. And a mission of kneeling there where the water is flowing kneeling, a chinese christian,

and let her think of a stable man and wandering and a repetition of counting. Count to ten. He did. He did not. Count to ten. And did she gather the food as well. Did she gather the food as well. Did she separate the green grasses from one another. They grow four times yearly. Did she see some one as she was advancing and did she remove what she had and did she lose what she touched and did she touch it and the water there where she was kneeling where it was flowing. And are stables a place where they care for them as well.

One might say that the essence of this passage is the phrase "as well"—a sort of welcome to anything that is there to come into the composition, such a welcome being the genius of France and as often as not of America. The coherence of the passage, which consists in a sort of melodic progress of consideration, is between the rational French discursiveness and the rambling American sympathy as Whitman had it. But more important is the kind of existence expressed here. The existence of the woman in the passage is intimately involved with the existence, growth, and movement of things in the landscape. Her kneeling and the water flowing and the grass growing four times yearly and the caring for Italians are all part of the same slow natural living of the place and the world.

III

In serious literary circles, as distinguished from the large public, Gertrude Stein's real accomplishments were always known. There, her influence was at one time considerable, though it worked in very different ways and degrees on different individuals. It was known that her writing had influenced, in certain respects, Sherwood Anderson and, later, Hemingway. It was supposed that Steinese had found echoes in Don Marquis' *archy and mehitabel* as well as in the difficult poetry of Wallace Stevens, who once wrote "Twenty men crossing a bridge,/ Into a village,/ Are/ Twenty men crossing a bridge/ Into a village." Her insistence on the primacy of phenomena over ideas, of the magnificence of sheer unmediated reality, found, one assumes, a rapturous response in Stevens, a quiet one in Marianne Moore. In *Axel's Castle*, Edmund Wilson's discriminating study of modern literature published as early as 1931, she had a chapter to herself, as had, in each case, Yeats, Valéry, Eliot, Proust, and Joyce. *Axel's Castle* was a decisive event in the history of modern reputations. Wilson had some doubts as to Gertrude Stein's readableness in certain books but few doubts as to her general importance. Steinese and its inventor had become reputable.

By the time she died, Gertrude Stein had become something she wanted still more to be—she called it "historical." As early as 1923, *Vanity Fair* had printed "Miss Furr and Miss Skeene," her wonderful, and easily intelligible, exhibit of the vocabulary of genteel Bohemianism—"Mr. Furr was quite a pleasant man. Helen Furr had quite a pleasant voice a voice quite worth cultivating." Beginning with *The Autobiography of Alice B. Toklas* (1932) she had developed unsuspected capacities for writing still more intelligibly. The universal surprise at this fact, combined with the intrinsic fascination of the book, made it a best seller. And dire though the *Autobiography* is with special pleading, with that whole invidious system of inclusions and exclusions described above, it remains one of the best memoirs in American literature.

The improvement in her literary status disturbed for a while her firm sense of herself and her place in the world. "Money is funny," she said quizzically as the royalties poured in. But she soon mastered her new role and played it with good-humored dignity. Returning to America for the first time since 1903, she lectured to sizable audiences across the country. And following World War II she became a kind of oracle and motherly hostess to American military personnel in liberated Paris. Just before her death her sayings and doings over there were much in the news in America; and her later writings, cast in a much modified Steinese, were sought by the popular magazines.

Gertrude Stein died in Paris in 1946 at the age of 72. She seems to have died at peace with herself, her natural craving for recognition to some extent satisfied. At least she died firmly in character, having delivered from her hospital bed the last specimen, and one of the most searching specimens, of Steinese. "What is the answer?" she inquired, and getting no answer said, laughing, "In that case, what is the question?"

1962

Memories
of James
Agee

James Agee died in May 1955 at the age of 45. His death was a great loss and grief to those who had known him, including myself (though I knew him only intermittently). But to me, at least, his death was not exactly a shock. Agee lived with a life-consuming sort of intensity. In the circles he frequented, everyone was pretty intense. They smoked, drank, talked, sat up late, wandered around the Village looking for company, dreamed of greatness, fought off sterility, just as he did. But it was more or less understood at the time that Agee was special. There was a unique energy in him just as there was a unique beauty in his voice, eyes and hands.

His intensity was different from that of others we knew. He smoked and drank as if to appease an elemental hunger rather than to satisfy a nervous craving. His talk was a sort of rite. Rarely a monologue, it was most often, and quite literally, *tête-à-tête*. At parties, among the swirling ranks, he liked to put his head together with some other sympathetic head, nodding emphatically all the time they talked, while he sliced, carved and scooped words out of the air with his hands. The subject was, usually, not some matter of general opinion but a particular thing: a Russian movie, FDR's oratory, an episode in Hawthorne or Joyce. The method was passionately analytical, the purpose was praise. Let us now

praise famous men. Argument was a false note in these confrontations. But it sometimes cropped up and he was capable
of rage, hard and soft at the same time, stone and moss. "Men
of letters are death, just death," he muttered in the course of
a long dispute I once had with him about some such writer—
was it Gide or Mann?

Mostly, though, he didn't dispute what you said; he refined on it. "Do you remember, Jim, how Edward G. Robinson gets shot down at the end of *Little Caesar?*" "Behind the
billboards, yes," Agee would reply, with slow meditative ec-
stasy; and then he would go on to re-create the whole scene in
amazing detail; the lighting of it, the sound made by the bul-
lets in the empty night, the helpless death slump of the
lonely little gangster. "*Little* Caesar he was—Charlie Chaplin turned criminal."

The topic was seldom abandoned until it had been treated
thoroughly. Meanwhile, your place as Agee's interlocutor
had probably been taken by other individuals in succession:
there were always eager candidates. At last the party would
have disintegrated—the aggrieved drunks have slouched
out, the political-minded have marched off in groups, still
debating—and there at 2 A.M. would be Agee with one interlocutor and two or three determined listeners, seated firmly
in his chair, consuming the last of the host's last bottle, duck-
ing his head, shaping his words with his hands, exhausting
the topic, exhausting his insatiable listeners, exhausting himself.

"Agee is a genius," a woman writer of decided opinions
once announced to a group of us. "Our *only* genius," she
added, looking hard at us. But "genius" is one of those class-
ifying words he resented. And if he *was* a genius, he was in
some sense a captive genius. He was a captive of the Luce

publications, for which he worked during long years. He was also the captive of an ideological age, in which he shone by contrast. Was he too comfortably uncomfortable in this position, occasionally snarling at his keepers but still accepting the ration of money or veneration they tossed into his cage, still on exhibit?

He had the sort of temperament which would have made him a great writer if he had been born just a little earlier. He belonged to the time of Fitzgerald, Hemingway, Faulkner, Cummings, Edmund Wilson. His own generation—it was to some extent mine as well—was as literary and ambitious as the older one. Agee, in particular, was very ambitious. But the younger ones seemed to lack the drive, the professional finesse, of the older ones. We tended to become something quite different: professional revolutionists, Freudians, Thomists, Southerners, journalists, critics, teachers. The authority that the older generation found in its literary talent, our generation found in systems of thought, political parties, business organizations, educational and other institutions, the examples of famous men. Yes, Agee's habit of praise, the piety that distinguished him from the reformist rancor of others, partly turned him inside out, too. It feasted to a considerable extent on what *had* been: his own past, the South's past, the recent past of art. As I make it out from his conversations and writings, his main struggle was to recapture a creativity which he associated with Joyce, Griffith, Chaplin and others. He labored to repossess a world that had been triumphantly realized by the modern masters.

If this is true, it helps to account for his piecemeal production as a writer, his occasional imitativeness and sentimentality, his difficulty in concentrating his mind on anything so definite as a story. Like Proust, he could only have *fully* realized himself in some super-work; but his *Remembrance of Things Past* remained unwritten.

What Agee did accomplish, between his movie reviews, his discursive but brilliant *Let Us Now Praise Famous Men,* his overwritten but moving short novel *The Morning Watch,* was magnificent, even though it seems fragmentary. I have space here to speak only of his posthumous novel, *A Death in the Family.*

As the publishers make clear in a note, the novel had to be assembled from a lot of manuscript left by the author when he died. The general subject is clear enough: the sudden death of a father and the consequences of it to his family, especially his small son. This central event, as well as the events immediately preceding it and immediately following from it, are accounted for in several chapters which appear finished. But there are six additional chapters, each more or less complete in itself, that deal with the same family, the same boy, but that do not seem either to presuppose or to anticipate the father's death. These chapters the editors have placed as best they could, printing them in italics. They have also included as a prelude a prose poem, "Knoxville: Summer 1915," which Agee published in *Partisan Review* twenty years ago.

A Death in the Family is, therefore, far from being a finished whole and it probably can't be understood or judged as such. It is, however, very wonderful in most of its parts. The jeweled prose that Agee sometimes resorted to elsewhere is occasionally, and disconcertingly, present here, too. There are also pages—including one that tries to render the noise of an auto starting—which sound too much like pages in *Ulysses.*

For the most part, however, the writing is in the colloquial

Mark Twain manner, which seems to come most naturally to Agee and which he makes fully his own, adding a certain richness of language and rhythm. An account of the family's visit to an ancient relative in the hills is in this style and is classic. So is the episode in which the son, Rufus, is bought a fancy cap by his aunt. He is essential boy and she is essential aunt and the cap is essential cap. As to the central subject, Agee renders the sheer shock of the death better than he renders any deeper realizations and consequences of it. Probably he would have got around to these: they seem to be assumed in *The Morning Watch,* which is about a similarly fatherless boy at a later stage of his development. *A Death in the Family* is incomplete, but it is full of superlative moments and confirms one's memories of the—literally—unforgettable man who wrote it.

1957

Literary
Comment

The
Duke's
Dilemma

The Life and Adventures of La Rochefoucauld is one of Morris Bishop's lively and learned biographies of historic Frenchmen. La Rochefoucauld, the seventeenth-century nobleman, soldier, lover, politician and author, is so brilliant a subject and Mr. Bishop presents him in such engaging detail that we remain convinced of the general worth of the book even when we dissent from some of its main conclusions.

La Rochefoucauld's story turns on one of those dilemmas which also preoccupied the dramatists of his time; in fact his story helps us to appreciate the elegant urgency of their plays. On the one hand he was possessed by a love of glory; on the other hand his glory could only be sustained by actions which inevitably diminished it. He was not in any foolish sense romantic or vain. His ambition had reference to that of his feudal family and class, both of which still enjoyed some power in France.

In the century of Richelieu and Louis XIV, however, that power was weakening; and no doubt the ambition of men like La Rochefoucauld was desperate in proportion as it was doomed. Their prestige had come to depend on privileges doled out by monarchs intent on consolidating their own power at the nobles' expense. La Rochefoucauld might protest that his glory was certified by his feudal past. In practice he had to engage in endless maneuvers in order that his wife should have the right of arriving at the Louvre door in her own carriage and of occupying a certain kind of stool in the queen's presence.

This was La Rochefoucauld's dilemma, which he tried to resolve in a life of action. In the course of it he resorted to almost every device of flattery, intrigue, seduction and open battle known to the time. Yet, in his capacity for self-awareness, for love and friendship, for wit, for gratuitous folly, and not least for boredom, he displayed an individual sensibility. If La Rochefoucauld harked back to the medieval hero Roland, he also foreshadowed the heroes of Stendhal. In him the great French ideal of *la gloire* was already fighting for its life.

His efforts largely failed. In the wars of the Fronde his castle was burned and he was almost blinded; his beloved natural son died in battle; his mistresses proved false; and in his poverty he had to marry his daughter to his former valet, now become rich. It was only when he turned to literature and friendship that he found any sort of lasting glory. By assisting Mme. de La Fayette to write her half-realistic stories of love and manners, he contributed to the inception of the modern novel, including of course the Stendhalian novel. And he wrote on his own the small bitter book of reflections by which he is chiefly known today. His shocked contemporaries received *The Maxims* as a classic and it has been one ever since. The work helped to fix French prose in its characteristic incisiveness; and it established La Rochefoucauld, in his concern with the psychology of self-interest, as the Machiavelli of the private life.

Dismayed by what he calls, without further qualification, their "cynicism," Bishop does not greatly admire *The Max-*

ims. And by incorporating a number of them into the text of
his story, he tries to show that they were the mere fruit of La
Rochefoucauld's personal disappointments. But the famous
sentences resist Bishop's ingenuity; they remain stoutly and
sometimes ludicrously unassimilated to the Duke's stream-of-
consciousness as it is imagined by his biographer. If Bishop's
experiment proves anything, it proves what Louis Kronenberger once suggested in his translation of *The Maxims:* that
they are the essentially impersonal product of a definite
method. This method Mr. Kronenberger defined as a "scientific cynicism . . . which tested vanity in a test-tube."

Meanwhile Bishop's account of the last years of La Rochefoucauld is full of grace and pity. The political rehabilitation
of the old nobleman was never to be complete. He was excluded from the Academy and declared unfit—as he doubtless was—to be tutor to the Dauphin. Yet when someone
presented the Dauphin with a gilded doll-house peopled by
effigies of the leading contemporary writers, it was noticed
that one of them represented La Rochefoucauld. Thus he
was finally established at court in all his glory, if only as a
doll.

1951

To Moscow
Again

"The profundity of Chekhov's works is inexhaustible to the actor," Stanislavsky said. But under present theater conditions, Chekhov's profundity, like Shakespeare's, can involve liabilities, for audience and actors alike. Perhaps it was so even in the patriarchal days of the archetypal Moscow Art Theater, Chekhov's shrine. There is evidence that things did not always go well there, although the playwright himself was at hand, or at least in Yalta, for consultation. He once complained that the officers' uniforms in *The Three Sisters* were too smart. The Russian military, he said, had ceased to be a glittering elite, had grown more cultured and shabbier. (The officers in *The Three Sisters* seem to have submitted wholly to the general bourgeoisifying trend, and the duel fought at the play's end, though fatal to one participant, is a travesty.)

But if the trouble was partly in the limitations to be found in any theater group, it was—and still is—largely in the profundity of Chekhov's art itself. While his plays were in rehearsal he was often asked by actors how such and such a scene or character should be done. And Chekhov, the kindliest of writers, would show a surprising impatience. "It's all there," he would reply. And no wonder. In his major plays, everything *is* there, in the script, from the state of people's souls at a given moment to the state of the weather. His exclusive reputation for small-scale effects is quite unfounded. The opposite is true of his effects. A principle of discreet but forceful expansion is at work in his major plays. Each interior implies an exterior. Often the exterior is a garden, and beyond the garden are fields, or streets and street crowds, all Russia, birds in flight, the succession of day and night, the seasonal cycle, Time, the universe. Nor is this almost epic range conveyed with any help from lengthy stage directions, like O'Neill's, or prefaces, like Shaw's. It's all there in the characters' talk, that munificent display of verbalism for which the term "dialogue" is a vulgar misnomer.

In her recent quarrel with the "theater arts" Establishment, in *The New York Review*, Elizabeth Hardwick insisted upon the primacy of literary talent in the theatrical process. "Drama is, after all, literature written for the stage," she said, and her claim seems to me incontrovertible. But if it needs any support it should find plenty in *The Three Sisters*, which is having a conscientious revival at the Morosco Theater in New York.

The usual Chekhovian profusion of detail swells into an immense opulence in this play. Farce and tragedy coalesce in an intricate, often bewildering, pattern of tonalities. The number of characters, each with his peculiar destiny to make manifest, his string of solo numbers to get off from time to time as he wanders on and off stage, is large. It is large, at least, by the standards of economy prevailing in the New York theater, where a cast is rarely numerous enough to get entangled, one with another, or with the furniture.

When the curtain goes up at the Morosco, the three sisters are all on stage, but only Olga, the eldest, and Irina, the youngest, are conversing. Masha, the other, is more or less supine on her famous sofa, book in hand, silent except for an occasional mocking whistle. This is the parsimonious privacy we are accustomed on the New York stage. But it doesn't last. Masha's body uncoils and her tongue loosens: she has some cutting observation to make. And pretty soon three officers appear at the back of the set, chatting casually beside a long table in what is the dining room. It is Irina's birthday. A luncheon party is under way. And now, one by one, the others materialize: Colonel Vershinin, the new battery commander, with whom Masha will fall in love; Andrey, the morose brother of the three girls; Natasha, his brash upstart of a fiancée; the aged army doctor who has forgotten all his medical knowledge, who drinks, and who is the voice of despair, Chekhov's gloomiest spokesman; and Solyony, a buffoon to end all Russian literary buffoons, who turns out to be a killer. Thus the stage is soon full and it will only rarely return to the original state of comparative privacy. In this community of spiritual doom privacy is unwanted. For all their despair and their antagonisms, Chekhov's characters are still Russians. As we know from their classic literature, Russians have—or *had*—a quality denied to most other modern peoples: a certain gregariousness of the soul. Russians love Russians.

In this community, moreover, no one is fully capable of living in the present. No one, that is, who has any sensibility at all. The rest are clowns, buffoons, or bitches, all of them as self-deceived and self-destructive in their own way as the sensitive people are in theirs. But if the latter are incapable of living in the present, they do live, with a dreamy, often mad, intensity, in the past or in the future. The sisters are always pining for Moscow, the lost Eden, once the family home, where the girls hope to live, really live, again. Vershinin perpetually conjures up the coming millennium, and his enthusiasm for it is matched by his reluctance to fix the date of its arrival. "And when more time has passed— another two or three hundred years . . . Oh, what a wonderful life that will be!"

Meanwhile there is much talk of salvation through work. The work idea is a kind of compromise between the nostalgia and the futurism. Some members of the circle do have jobs. There are the schools to be staffed, and the army, the telegraph office, the administrative positions at the County Board. Between the jobs and the people who work at them, however, the disparity is in most cases total. So actual work doesn't pay off either, spiritually speaking. And therefore they talk and talk, creating themselves in conversation—if conversation is the word for the wonderfully disjointed flow of remark that goes on in the play: the irrelevancies, the non-sequiturs, the garbled quotations, the bad French and juvenile Latin, the animal cries, and—as a last resort—the forays into seeming nonsense. The verbalism of the play finds its ultimate form in nonsense. Solyony, the buffoon and future killer, torments his prospective victim with cries of "chook, chook, chook." Masha and Vershinin like to communicate by means of a sort of Slavic love call that goes "Tram-tam-tam." The old doctor voices his gentle despair in the syllables of the Offenbachian refrain: "Tarara-boom-de-ay." This phrase he hums softly to himself just before the final curtain falls. Famous last words. Tragedy into farce.

Thus the people seek salvation in talk, among other things. And thus *The Three Sisters*, considered as "literature written for the stage," finds its special language in their fantastic style. Paradoxically, however, its structure is determined, not by what they do but, for the most part, by what they don't do—by their habit of inaction or, at most, of action that is compulsive and unconsidered.

At their level, in fact, the usual distinctions between action and inaction, conscious will and sentient passivity, disappear as they do in dreams. And Chekhov, one of the chief progenitors of the modern tradition in drama, comes close to some of its most recent exponents, the Absurdists, as they may be called. Between the people who pine for Moscow and the people who wait for Godot, a family resemblance is detectable. In both groups there is a great urgency of salvation, and a professed belief that salvation is to be found, not really in work or talk, but in a dream of transcendence: the going to Moscow, the coming of Godot. In both, finally, there is a profound suspicion that this belief is illusory. Quite literally, they hope against hope. Thus it might be said that Beckett's people are merely Chekhov's people dispossessed of their furniture and stripped down to their reflexes. The former are dehumanized, the latter over-humanized, but the essential predicament is the same. For Chekhov's people, at any rate, the things that make up their humanity also constitute the symptoms of their failure. Their learning, their sensibility, their gentility, even their knowledge of the polite languages, are a burden to them. Their culture exists only that it may be forgotten, leaving them with the wistful pleasure of forever mourning its loss. "I've even forgotten the Italian for window, or ceiling," Irina remarks, apropos of nothing in particular and everything in general.

Yet one must avoid seeing Chekhov's work, and Beckett's for that matter, too exclusively in the light of such affinities and continuities. The works of both are far from being mere versions of moral history, mere stages in the evolution or devolution of humanism. To speak only of Chekhov: his sofas are as essential to his conception of life as they are to his stage sets, and so are the other amenities implied by the sofas. It was as a realist, however visionary, that he conceived his characters and wrote his plays, while Beckett, as I understand him, is a pure visionary of the "Absurd."

In its form and genre, too, *The Three Sisters* belongs to the end of the age of realism. It is a bourgeois melodrama *manqué*. The principals refuse to enact the roles assigned them by the original genre. Many of the original situations are present. The son of the family marries an ambitious village wench. He contracts gambling debts. The home is mortgaged. There are loveless marriages and adulterous goings-on. There is the duel. By degrees, the ambitious wench succeeds in largely dispossessing the family. The keys to the larder end by dangling from her belt rather than, as formerly, from that of Olga, the rightful chatelaine. In *The Three Sisters*, however, the family really dispossesses itself. The usual confrontations of melodrama fail to occur. What is lacking is not so much the will to resist aggression as the concentration of feeling needed to bring the will into play. Feeling is not absent, of course. It is all over the place. There are embraces, protestations, citations from the poets, flights of philosophy, and tears, tears, tears. But this tangle of emotions is unable to attach itself to any set of objects at all fitting. It thus fails to stimulate the will and to serve as a guide to conduct. The emotional confusion confuses the practical issues for the family members, even while investing those individuals with pathos and charm. In one of the few scenes that verge on a real confrontation, Olga is finally roused to anger against her brother's wife, Natasha. But it is not for her machinations, or even her affair with a leading citizen, that

Natasha is brought to book. It is because in a fit of temper she has spoken harshly to an old servant. "The very slightest rudeness, a tactless word upsets me," Olga cries. Her sensitivity to rudeness is admirable. One loves her for it. But in the light of the whole family situation, it falls quite short of the mark. It reminds us, and Natasha, of Olga's superior gentility but it doesn't get the house back.

1964

Thomas
Mann

I. The Good European

If all novelists are in some degree social historians, Thomas Mann was the great novelist-historian of the present crisis in Western culture. He made a magnificent spectacle out of what has since become a sad and desperate routine. Between the unlovely facts of disease and death on the one hand, and the glories of art and philosophy on the other, he discovered a metaphysical affinity. For Mann, and for his early readers, there was a sort of beauty in the contemplation of this affinity. It lent a grandeur to the slow disintegration of the Buddenbrooks, the rapid fall of Aschenbach in "Death in Venice," the up-and-down career of Hans Castorp in *The Magic Mountain*. Today, when the pressure of those unlovely facts and of the whole ever-worsening crisis seems to outweigh any current achievements in art and philosophy, Mann's metaphysics seem unconvincing.

Indeed, despite all his concern with decadence, there was in Thomas Mann an old-fashioned interest in soul cures, and an old-fashioned art went with it. The possibility of a cure was firmly implied in the story, even when the suggested cure failed to work for the hero in question. The cure consisted partly in an exposure to new experience, such as falling ill, falling in love, and traveling; partly in a submission to Socratic procedures: scarcely a novel or tale of Mann's is without some simulacrum of a Socratic dialogue in the course of which the hero's inherited ideas are subjected to intensive scrutiny by himself and others. The unexamined life is not worth living.

Mann's faith in the reality of ideas was profound. So was his genius for seeing ideas written large and grand, or small and droll, in the drama of human character, of manners, and of history. The peculiar attraction of his work—for a past generation that *did* find it attractive—lay in the relation of its drama to its ideas, its surface to its interior. The surface teems with anecdote: no modern novelist has given us more characters, happenings, and scenes that have the immediate charm of first-rate anecdote; while the interior is alive with dim but active intellectual presences: Spirit and Nature, Democracy and Aristocracy, North and South, and so on. The art of Mann consisted in fusing the surface with the interior, in thoroughly crystallizing the anecdotes into universal parables.

Nowadays it is often objected that all this is overdone in Mann's work. The crystallizing process is *too* thorough, the symbolism employed to accomplish it too obtrusive, the whole art of the man too surgically expert and complacently omniscient. To be sure, similar objections were heard even in the heyday of his reputation. There was always some doubt as to the ultimate creative intensity of his mind as compared with his greatest contemporaries in the novel. To go from Mann to Joyce or Proust or Kafka was, one said, like passing through the frame into the picture, or exchanging the doctor's office for the confessional. For what they are worth, these distinctions make sense now as they did in the past; and Mann has been under the further disadvantage that his complex German did not go into very acceptable English. Thus he has exerted far less influence than Joyce or Proust or Kafka on writing in this country. He has been the intelligent reader's novelist rather than the novelist's novelist.

The objections to Mann's work have become sharper in recent years. For beyond the merely technical criticisms lies a changed point of view upon literature and life—a change begotten, evidently, not by any lessening of the crisis in culture but by its vastly greater gravity. Mann's faith in ideas, his passion for explanations, have given way to an ethos of the Cool, of moral ingenuousness, in life as in literature. The *examined* life is not worth living.

It takes a really free-spirited critic to rehabilitate a dated classic. Mann is such a classic now and Mark Van Doren is such a critic; and Mr. Van Doren's small recent book on *Joseph and His Brothers* showed what could come of an encounter between such a pair. Where most critics have been engulfed by Mann's own omnivorous critical intelligence, Van Doren remains serenely visible. Between the German novelist with his elegant complexity and the American critic with his elegant simplicity there is a dramatic half-meeting of minds. It takes place, moreover, on Van Doren's chosen ground: the theory and practice of comedy. Thus one critic has made this dated writer his own, just as others may well in time make him theirs.

Here, meanwhile, are two further books on the subject, one about Mann, the other by him. Erich Heller's *The Ironic German* is a study of Mann's mind and work; and it has the immediate purpose, one gathers, of refurbishing Mann's image in the public mind. Mann's *Last Essays,* containing four literary portraits written during his later years, is a very personal and quite moving volume full of what appear to be tacit reflections on Mann's image as it came to exist in his own mind.

Anyone who is already familiar with his work will find comfort and instruction in *The Ironic German*. Mr. Heller's account of the novelist's intellectual composition and affinities is thorough; his defense of Mann in the dialogue that forms his chapter on *The Magic Mountain* is spirited; his analyses of the major works are excellent even though a little too lengthy and tortuous for what they contain. The point of view on Mann is not, however, very fresh or even very clear and well sustained. Unlike Mr. Van Doren, Mr. Heller does tend to fall victim to Mann's omnivorous mind, or at least to the similarities between their two minds.

For one thing, Mr. Heller's title seems unfortunate, almost a caricature. The "ironic" suggests a pose rather than a man and the "German" fastens on a world artist the fatalism of race. In part the book itself corrects the first of these impressions, showing that Mann's irony served a "moral intelligence" of the first order. Yet Mr. Heller is ultimately a little uncomfortable with the irony and with its philosophic basis. By way of gently suggesting Mann's supposed limitations, he cites Kierkegaard and his famous hierarchy of Being. Mann's early hero, Tonio Kröger, and by implication Mann himself, are said to have occupied "that border-region between the aesthetic and the ethical state" which lies considerably below the ultimate or religious state. But anybody can cite Kierkegaard and nowadays almost everybody does. The question is whether Kierkegaard is relevant to Mann, an uncompromising theist to an uncompromising humanist.

Then there is the difficulty of Mann's Germanism. Given Mr. Heller's background as a self-exiled writer of Middle Eu-

ropean origins, and his position as an authority on German
literature and thought, it is natural that he should see Mann
largely in the light of their common traditions. And Mr.
Heller undoubtedly contributes a great deal of subtly rea-
soned evidence to the study of Mann's antecedents. Yet
Mann's conscious debt to, his veritable identification with,
such figures as Goethe, Schopenhauer, Wagner and Nietzsche, are explored in *The Ironic German* to the point where
one sometimes feels that one is participating in a mystery
rather than reading about a novelist.

Concerning Mann's famous idea of the Bourgeois, Mr.
Heller characteristically writes: "It seems an elusive but
powerful organism capable of absorbing into its indefinitely
expansive system a vast variety of incommensurable things:
a measure of German piety and a measure of Will to Power,
Goethe's doctrine of resignation and Nietzsche's dithyrambic
excesses, Stifter's untempestuous ideal and Wagner's musical
demon, Schopenhauer's will to saintliness and Bismarck's
Realpolitik." Thus are Mann's many ghostly forebears sum-
moned by Mr. Heller from their widely scattered graves. No
wonder he concludes that Mann practiced a sort of "*Imitatio
mystica*" of the dead, hoping thus to leave behind "a body of
work which could truly claim to be the parodistic résumé of
German Literary History."

But true as this may be, does it account for the living
force and variety of Mann's work? Are not his German pi-
eties a part of his private history as distinguished from whatever it was that made him a great novelist of modern experience? And is it not just as a great novelist of modern
experience that his image needs to be refurbished?

The *Last Essays* evoke a less past-haunted Thomas Mann
than we sometimes get from *The Ironic German*, despite its

excellence in other respects. And although three of Mann's subjects in this book were German—they are Schiller, Goethe, and Nietzsche, the fourth and most reverently portrayed is Chekhov—the book recalls us to Mann's character as the German become the "Good European." Indeed, Nietzsche's famous formula seems to have been invented just for Mann, in this final phase as in most of his writing after *The Magic Mountain.* The *Last Essays* also reminds us of Mann's old genius as an essayist, his way of combining his extraordinary powers of intellectual analysis with his novelist's gift of creating characters and telling stories.

But what lends a peculiar interest to these characters and stories is the extent to which they add up to a gentle inquisition on his own character, life, and work. For one thing he seems to change sides, writing very warmly about Schiller and Chekhov, two figures who were in many ways his opposite numbers, and writing rather less sympathetically of Goethe and Nietzsche, a pair with whom he had formerly identified himself quite closely. "In Germany greatness tends to a kind of hypertrophy," he remarks in "Fantasy on Goethe," the last of his several studies of that poet. And he goes on to show how Goethe "had in his majestic old age a good deal of this absolutism and personal imperialism," and how "at his death there was to be heard not only the nymphs' lament for great Pan, but a distinct 'Whew' of relief." Nor does Mann spare us any of Nietzsche's vulgarity and brutality in his brilliant but perhaps too immediately political reconsideration of that figure, "Nietzsche in the Light of Recent History."

On the other hand, Schiller and Chekhov are praised for their relative humility and their steady devotion to principle. Where Nietzsche's fatal illness is related not only to his triumphs as a thinker but to his megalomaniac excesses, Chekhov's illness is said to have produced a "strange, skeptical and infinitely endearing modesty." He was, Mann says, "too modest even for passion." After all, Chekhov was a *real* doctor and knew too much about disease to glorify it as Nietzsche did and Mann after him. What Chekhov accomplished in the short story, a form that Mann says he himself scorned in his youth, is contrasted favorably with "works of monumental stature"—surely works like some of Mann's own. And Chekhov's narrative art is roundly declared to be (as it undoubtedly is) "unsurpassed in European literature." Yet, as Mann is at pains to show, Chekhov became a great artist more or less by accident: through the intervention of a forgotten Russian critic who saw promise in his early journalistic sketches. Here again there is an implied contrast, this time with Mann's own conception of the artist as an historically and metaphysically predestined entity.

It is in his account of Chekhov's ultimate beliefs, or lack of them, that the essay is most intimately revealing of the author's state of mind. A thinker ought to answer the question "What is to be done?" Chekhov believed; yet he could not say what was to be done to improve conditions in Czarist Russia or ameliorate the human condition in general. He did not, however, take refuge in irony or dialectical exercises but ruefully sought, as he said, "just to depict life as it is, without taking one step further." In other words, Chekhov avowed his uncertainties more clearly and humbly than Mann himself had ever done.

But it is not the implied self-criticism that matters in these essays so much as the impulse behind it. Despite his years, his fame, his achievement, Thomas Mann could still suffer, still reflect, still play Socrates to his own ideas. Like Chekhov, he lived to be greatly tried by personal ordeals, fearfully depressed by the state of the world; and both men sought relief in visions of a "perhaps imminent day when life will be bright and joyful as a peaceful Sunday morning." The words are Chekhov's but the dream is both Chekhov's and Mann's. Thus a writer as enormously complex as Mann had always been, and as complacent in his greatness as he had sometimes seemed, was capable at last of visions and other simplicities! This strange and wonderful fact underlies the *Last Essays* and gives them their peculiar preciousness. It also points to the more-than-German, the better-than-ironical, the magnificently universal artist that remains to be rediscovered in Mann's work as a whole.

1959

II. Thomas Mann's Farewell

Another substantial volume in black and gold has been added to the long shelf-full of such volumes that make up Thomas Mann's work for American readers. No doubt the present volume will be the last. Mann's works, like his days, have ended. They have ended well: *Confessions of Felix Krull, Confidence Man,* is an amusing comedy of ideas, a richly documented historical fantasy, and Mann's finest performance since *Doctor Faustus.*

The book had been gestating in the novelist's mind for many years. The early chapters were written as far back as 1911. Further chapters were added some ten years later, and the resulting fragment has long been familiar to us by reason of its inclusion among Mann's shorter writings in *Stories of Three Decades.* He spent his last years expanding the tale

into a sizable affair. Even now, we have only the first install-
ment of a narrative which could have continued more or less
indefinitely, provided that the author had lived to continue
it. But it doesn't matter that *Felix Krull* is still formally incomplete, that the hero, impersonating the Marquis de Ve-
nosta, has yet to embark on his projected world travels.
Mann's is the kind of picaresque story that tends to complete itself as it proceeds.

True to its type, *Felix Krull* is the story of a rogue's progress. From small beginnings as the offspring of a ruined
Rhineland family, the hero goes on to cut a figure in the
great world of Paris and beyond. His career is a succession of
amiable ruses, thefts and seductions. Above all, it is a series
of impersonations, for Krull is disgusted with his own identity and constantly seeks to exchange it for others. He even
enacts a sick man—and does it so enthusiastically that his
draft board is fooled into rejecting him for the German
Army. Finding work in a fashionable Paris hotel, he is by
turns the perfect elevator boy, the perfect waiter, the perfect
thief, the perfect lover. A gushing poetess whom he has
robbed of some of her jewels finds him so remarkable a bed-
mate that, on learning of the theft, she gives him the rest of
her jewels. A Scottish lord, smitten in his way by Krull, seeks
to adopt him and make him his heir. But Krull disengages
himself from the insistent poetess and refuses the enamored
lord. He seems to be saving himself for something—for the
perfect adventure, it appears. And presently something of
this kind offers itself. A young Luxembourgian nobleman
whose parents wish him to make a world tour has his reasons
for preferring to remain in Paris. He bestows his name, rank,
and ample letter of credit on the willing Krull, who then sets
off for South America.

Mann's hero is the pretext for some admirable episodes, but he is not very interesting in himself. He seems just a little dated. His intellectual paraphernalia of masks and roles, the ironic glitter of his accomplished naughtiness, declare him to be a contemporary of Shaw's Don Juan, Gide's Lafcadio and other heroes of that Nietzsche-haunted age. It was a notable age, but to return to it by way of Mann's belated fantasy is to feel that it is distinctly distant and that the book itself is a period-piece. While reading it, one consents to play the Zarathustran as one might consent, at a costume party, to dance the tango in a ballroom conscientiously furnished with specimens of Art Nouveau. One knows all the time that it doesn't mean a thing.

The author himself seems to have felt this upon taking up *Felix Krull* again in his old age. Young or old, he was always intelligent, always resourceful; and it is a part of the book's endless game of impostures that the aged Mann is willfully impersonating the younger Mann. Thus Krull's later adventures are more broadly farcical than his earlier ones, and the atmosphere of psychological motivation and meaning has thinned. At the same time, the spirit of *pastiche* has grown franker. Krull is now reminiscent by turns of Rousseau, Casanova, Mr. Yorick, Rameau's Nephew and several other classic scamps of autobiography and fiction. Mann has even seen to it that he writes his confessions in a sober, sententious prose which recalls that of Goethe's *Wilhelm Meister*. Come to think of it, Krull and his adventures are not so much dated as simply historical. They form a sort of animated Mme. Tussaud's, although the exhibit is clearly contrived by a waxworker of genius.

In his authoritative little book on Mann, Henry Hatfield observes that the original Felix Krull belonged in Mann's gallery of portraits of the artist. Krull, says Mr. Hatfield, is "the artist as mountebank." For the later Mann, however, this hero seems to have been largely a pretext for abandoning himself to the pleasures of sheer invention. And barring the scenes of passion—here, as in *The Holy Sinner,* the frisky sensuality of the aged Mann is awful—his contrivances are brilliant. When Krull, posing as the Marquis, writes a long dutiful letter to the real Marquis's mother, and receives from her a lengthy reply, full of a serene and pedantic nobility, the writing is equal to Mann's in his heyday.

And for old devotees of his work there is a fascination in the way he returns in *Felix Krull* to his well-known themes and preoccupations. The familiar young man, from Lübeck or Hamburg or the land of Canaan, who takes leave of his family, breaks with his confining native circumstances and fares forth into the big alien world, is reincarnated in Felix Krull, though with less than the usual solemnity. And with the reappearance in full dress of Mann's old theme there is a resurgence of his old special skills and knowledges. One last time he rejoices in what he knows of the ways of hotels and restaurants, the rituals of travel, the feel of foreign places, the forms of class behavior and racial manners, the whole comedy of cosmopolitanism. By consenting merely to simulate creation, he accomplishes in *Felix Krull* something like the real article. "How inventive life is!" declares the hero. How inventive, to the last, was Thomas Mann.

1955

The
Imagination
of Duchesses

The novelist who writes familiarly of dukes and duchesses
has a special burden of proof to discharge. He must persuade
us that he really knows his privileged characters, that they
are worth knowing, and that they are at once like and unlike
ourselves. What he requires, in short, is a knowledge of them
in their common human nature as well as in the remarkable
forms that human nature may assume when it is combined
with uncommon privilege. Proust excelled at this complex in-
sight; his portraits of the *beau monde* are vivid with it; he
was a master of the double exposure. In no other novelist are
there more amazing exhibitions of privileged human nature.

A la Recherche du temps perdu is something besides a
novel of social history. It is a portrait of the artist, a story of
how he achieves his vocation, an account of the processes by
which his imagination is delivered from its bondage to time
and passion. The other characters, however compelling in
themselves, are all securely drawn into the orbit of this central preoccupation. They may or may not be artists but they
have distinct creative endowments, and it is on their use or
misuse of these endowments that their several stories turn.
To be human for Proust is above all to have imagination.

I use the word in the sense that he appears to have had in

Originally a paper read before the English Institute.

mind when, writing to a friend, he described snobbishness as "a wonderful kind of imagination." In *A la Recherche du temps perdu* not only snobbishness but jealousy and other passions are seen as wonderful kinds of imagination. Imagination is as necessary to Proust's characters as generators are to automobiles. The generator converts mechanical into electrical energy, making the horn sound and the headlights shine. Imagination registers our desires and translates them into surprising forms of thought, speech and action. In this respect the men and women of *A la Recherche du temps perdu* are highly specialized. Whether they are duchesses, doctors, or procurers, the energy of desire is magnificently marked in them and so is the energy of mental invention.

In actual life, they would probably pass for geniuses. They *are* geniuses of a sort, even though most of them squander their endowment in a world of delusion. The power of invention is obvious and terrible in the major figures; it is also striking in cases where it is quite unexpected or is thoroughly malapropos—in short, where the effect of it tends to be comic. Such is the case of the very literal-minded Dr. Cottard with his outrageous puns; of Odette de Crécy with her small anxious lies and her brave show of Anglomania; of the elevator boy's sister who expresses her contempt for the poor by defecating on them in some unspecified manner; of the man who says he owns a painting by Rubens and then, when asked if it is signed, insists he cut off the signature to make the picture fit a frame that was already in his possession!

Montaigne observed that when the mind is insufficiently occupied "it brings forth many chimeras and fantastic monsters." Montaigne was referring to the intellectual dangers of being alone and idle; Proust finds such dangers in the busiest social life. The drawing room breeds its own chimeras. The abuse of imagination, the making it project selfish desire rather than seek out truth, is for Proust a very condition of social intercourse when pursued for its own sake. His worldly characters tend not only to think up monsters but, in doing so, to become monsters.

If, therefore, we compare Proust's idea of society with that of the great nineteenth century French novelists we see that a shift has occurred in the relations of the one and the many. Persons of marked imaginative powers were the exceptions in Balzac, Stendhal, and Flaubert. They were, or supposed themselves to be, the chosen few; and it was just the singularity of their minds and aims that made their adventures worth recording. Lucien de Rubempré, Julien Sorel, Emma Bovary—each may covet money or power or sexual adventure as other people covet those things; but in doing so each is essentially intent on realizing some idea he has of himself. We know, moreover, that it is usually from their reading, in romances or heroic memoirs, that they have learned the roles they propose to play. Each has in some fashion studied his part before embarking on his adventures; their indebtedness to literature makes clear how exceptional their aspirations are. And what are their adventures but a succession of collisions between their adopted roles and the hard surfaces of the social generality? Such is the impact for Julien Sorel that he can only maintain his idea of himself by finally courting imprisonment and death, while Emma Bovary sees her dreams succumb gradually to the prevailing materialism— sees them turn, as it were, into commodities: sheer sex, mere furniture, poplin by the yard.

The exceptional souls have taken over society in Proust's conception of it. Money-making, career-making, matchmaking and the other practical enterprises that provided the older novel with its characteristic intrigues are in the background of *A la Recherche du temps perdu*. The old struggle for tangible ends has given place to an all but universal struggle for prestige, and even this value seems precariously subjective, the stuff of ignorant supposition and willful desire. What almost everyone in Proust is intent upon is the projection of the self; this is now the enterprise of the many rather than of the distinguished few. There is, to be sure, the estimable Dr. Cottard who frequents the drawing room to further his career as a society physician ("plus de diagnostique Potain"); but it is Cottard's performance in the drawing room that matters. He too is "in society"—is there to shine as he believes a society doctor should shine. His literal mind flowers in its own fashion. He shines by his brusque, probing habits of speech and the painful surgery of his terrible puns. The various servants are in society too by reason of their occupations; Françoise, the chief of them, has her vivid ideas of herself; and we recall how brilliantly the haughty *"marquise"* of the W.C. in the Champs Elysées exemplifies the general condition.

The seekers of self are many and various in the novel, and so are their ways of representing themselves to the world. Each has a distinct quality of taste, a certain style of life, which he believes to be essential to the winning of prestige. Mme. Verdurin has her muscular music-lover's style, the foreign minister Norpois his musty diplomatic clichés and woolly Machiavellianism, Albertine her touching athlete's idiom, the young Marquise de Cambremer her determined patter of the person with advanced views on the arts. And though they all think of themselves as very special, even unique, they hasten to make common cause with others of similar style. They band together in protective and aggressive coteries based on the community of ideas. I refer, of course, to those characters who are definitely *dans le monde;* there are others—the painter Elstir, the narrator's grandmother—who cultivate their distinctive idioms and ideas of themselves in a wholly different spiritual climate.

Oriane, duchesse de Guermantes, is not only *in* the world, she *is* the world—in her own and certain other people's eyes. Her powers of imagination are limited but they are acute, and she is one of Proust's exemplary characterizations. In a medium where all is flux, she has the distinction of being relatively stable. Despite some vital changes in her nature and position, Mme. de Guermantes goes on and on.

On one occasion she is entertaining her dinner guests at the expense of an absent woman acquaintance when M. de Guermantes interrupts her. "Gad, Oriane," he explodes, "after all she's a duchess." Mme. de Guermantes feels the rebuke and falls silent. Several times in the course of the narrative the Duke thus calls her to order and she falls silent. Considering her usual effrontery, these are significant and somehow poignant moments. Her wit, so dear to her vanity and usually to her husband's, must give way to considerations of rank; and without her wit she is speechless, though never for long. Between her nature and her position there is a contradiction. She rejoices in a critical sensibility which exercises itself on all occasions and all comers. It is her pleasure to administer small shocks to the moral complacency of princesses, to take Tolstoy's side against visiting Russian grand dukes. Yet she is a member of a circle which constitutes her medium just as water is the medium of fish. Though chafing sometimes at its restrictions, she is unthinkable without it. She may imagine herself to be a free spirit but she is entirely a creature of contingencies. And when she surrenders to her husband it is not because she loves him—there is no affection between them—but because he is the living embodiment of the principle of necessity in her life. Faithless, brutal, stupid, he nevertheless represents the facts of money and rank without which she cannot operate.

To describe the Duke's incarnation of these things, Proust resorts to a comic exaggeration of his own grand manner, including the usual reference to the work of art. "Next to her, heavily seated, was M. de Guermantes, superb and Olympian. The sense of his vast riches seemed to be omnipresent in all his members and gave him a peculiar high density, as though he had been melted in a crucible into a human ingot to form this man who was worth so much. . . . I seemed to see that statue of Olympian Zeus which Phidias, they say, made all of gold."

Living with such a work of art is naturally uncomfortable for the Duchess but she cannot live without it. For she is like all the Guermantes family, and in a sense like all Proust's characters, in that she is possessed of a quality beyond her immediate social needs. There is a purposiveness about her which is in excess of the practical requirements of her position. Her great name, unlimited funds, considerable beauty, and unsullied reputation are enough in themselves to sustain her supreme position in the Faubourg Saint-Germain. Yet her special quality of imagination, her idea of herself, demands that she play a role enacted by no one else.

The Courvoisiers, a family of lay figures which Proust introduces for purposes of comparison with the Guermantes, are content with the actualities of their equally fine position. They are resigned to being what their status calls for, even if it means being rather dull. Oriane de Guermantes must be a wit to boot, must be in fact unique.

In this demand she resembles other members of the Guermantes family, all of whom are shown to share a peculiar type of *esprit*. One of them reads Nietzsche and aspires to be an intellectual. Another has had Bohemian adventures and is engaged in writing her memoirs. The greatest of them, the Baron de Charlus, is driven to elaborate perversities, cruelties, impostures. Primarily he has, along with his genuine endowments, an extravagant sense of his own privileged position. His gifts of mind entitle him, provided he translate them into a vocation, to legitimate privileges as a creative intelligence. With his knowledge of society, his eloquence, his original moral stamina, he might be, say, the Tacitus of his generation. But he fails to realize his artistic gifts; he confuses them with the virtues which supposedly inhere in his social position. In proportion as he fails to get the right kind of recognition, he demands more and more of the wrong kind. His defeatism in wartime, which Proust describes in penetrating detail in the last volume, represents the ultimate effort of his imagination in its political character. Starved for *his* kind of prestige, Charlus can finally envision the destruction of the nation that denies it to him. And meanwhile his homoerotic fantasies have turned frankly self-destructive. Instead of being a Tacitus, he has come to resemble one of Tacitus' malevolent emperors. He is a Nero of the imagination.

The Duchess' smaller range causes her to have a fate less drastic than her brother-in-law's. As time goes on, she merely sharpens and dwindles. Her wit, thoroughly charming at a time when it was stimulated by that of her friend Swann, grows coarser, crueler, more animalistic, more showy. We never see her from the inside; she has no private life save by implication. Still, we know her to be suffering more and more from her husband's brutality and from the fatigue of going round and round in her vicious circle. Her own pain leads her to give pain to others: to torment her servants, to forget her dying friends, to hasten their oblivion once they are dead, to dismiss from her mind the thought of death itself. She needs constantly to demonstrate her supposed freedom of spirit by exercising it in novel ways and so begins to consort with the Bohemian circles she had formerly despised. At last, when it is too late, she finds herself virtually outside that Faubourg Saint-Germain which was her natural province and only true arena. If the fish formerly scorned the water, the water now shuns the fish.

Yet Mme. de Guermantes retains always something of her original grace and gaiety and genius for fashion. She continues to exhibit some of the refinement that is the inalienable privilege of the Guermantes. And so do the other characters retain something of their original energy. *A la Recherche du temps perdu* is about men and art, and for Proust the world of art is continuous with that of other men. Social intercourse *for its own sake* is vanity, but people in society are distinguished by energy, eloquence, connoisseurship and a high evaluation of themselves. These qualities form a link between them and the mind of the artist. One of the paintings by Elstir, Proust's imaginary great Impressionist, shows the land and the sea partaking of the same substance and composing a reality superior to both. A similar interpenetration of values—social, moral, aesthetic—characterizes Proust's general sense of life. Everywhere in the novel, amid all the misery and corruption, there are occasions for beauty, intimations of immortality: Mme. de Guermantes's red shoes, the carnations that Odette's horses wear on their blinkers while her coachman wears a matching one in his lapel, the basket of fruit that Swann assembles lovingly from the various shops specializing in the several kinds of fruit—the peach here, the pear there, the grapes someplace else. Lionel Trilling has remarked that a reader of nineteenth century French novels, with their relentless social criticism, might be tempted to conclude that "society is a fraud." It would be a singularly unwary reader who would conclude as much from Proust's novel.

1955

The Coming
of Nabokov

I. A Preface to Lolita

In *Lolita* Vladimir Nabokov has made a notable tale out of
notably forbidding matter and breathed fresh virulence into
the great tradition, recently languishing, of the *roman noir*.
The author of several novels, a first-rate memoir of his Russian childhood and exilic youth, a cranky study of Gogol, and
some learned monographs on the subject of *Lepidoptera*, Mr.
Nabokov is an experienced and no doubt widely read man of
letters. But none of his previous ventures has quite prepared
us for the impact of *Lolita*. The impact of *Lolita* on American publishers—the several who saw it in manuscript—was
such that the book was finally brought out by a small press in
Paris. American publishers are not greatly to blame. There is
a real challenge in *Lolita,* and to say there is not would do
the book itself an injustice. A largely sympathetic critic writing in *Partisan Review* (Mr. John Hollander) declares that
Lolita "flames with a tremendous perversity of an unexpected kind." It does, and the flame would definitely singe a
sleeve; and for just this reason *Lolita* is not for the mere fan-
cier of erotica or consumer of pornography, if there are such
people and if they matter. *Lolita* applies its heat to the entire
sensibility, including the sense of humor. Instead of putting
the desires in an agreeable simmer, it acts on them almost
like a cautery, sterilizing them with horrid laughter. Be-

tween the horror and the hilarity of it, *Lolita* is a fascinating but very special sort of experience. It is a tale for the adult public; and should it sometime be published in the United States, it could be trusted, I think, to make its mark with that public as an original work of literature.

Meanwhile Mr. Nabokov's terrible infant circulates over here in its Paris format, gets itself reviewed in advanced periodicals and acquires a small celebrity. But this celebrity, if it is of the kind I think it is, could do the book a subtler injury than censorship can do, insisting as it mostly does that *Lolita* is no more than a very brilliant joke or literary burlesque. Mr. Hollander gives good reason for being of this opinion. He suggests that the book has, besides its tremendous perversity, a wealth of uproarious parody but "no clinical, sociological or mythic seriousness."

Lolita is very funny, very full of burlesque intentions, but the supreme laugh may be on the reviewers for failing to see how much of everyone's reality lurks in its fantastic shadow play. Surely the ways listed by Mr. Hollander—clinical, sociological, mythic—are not the only ways of making perversity pay off in literature; there are simpler ways of being serious. Mr. Nabokov has devoted much art to making *Lolita* yield reactions which I can only describe as "human." True, his hero is a thorough creep and no pitiable sick man or aspiring sick soul. He is contrived in such a way that he resists the charity of the clinic and refuses to be vaporized into allegory. Entangled in some of the most intricately sordid situations ever presented by a novelist, his hero tends to be in fact what some of Joyce's characters become in their guilty fantasies: a "sex fiend" pursued by angry bodies of righteous citizens. Incongruously, however, his situations are always assuming familiar forms, his horrid scrapes become our scrapes. The book's general effect is profoundly mischievous, like that of some diabolical distorting mirror in some particularly obscene amusement park. The images of life that *Lolita* gives back are ghastly but recognizable. If Mr. Nabokov's methods are the usual methods of comedy, they are here carried to new extremes.

Lolita purports to be the confession of a man who is in confinement awaiting trial for murder. But Humbert Humbert, as the hero-narrator calls himself, has something besides murder on his mind. He is attracted solely to "nymphets," girls of about twelve to fifteen years; and this anomaly of his nature, which has ended by ruining him, has also come close to destroying Lolita, his stepdaughter who at the age of twelve became his lover. Humbert begins by trying to account for his obsession. He refers us back to his childhood in Europe (he is a Swiss citizen but "a salad of racial genes") and to the small girl with whom he had an affair that was constantly disrupted by adult intruders and finally terminated forever by the girl's early death. Humbert is—or half thinks he is—a victim of interrupted coitus, and he continues to pursue the dead girl's image among the indifferent nymphets of the world. A regular marriage to a "life-sized woman" in Paris ends ridiculously, and Humbert makes his way to America. The time is the late 1940s.

Here, in a small New England town, he falls in with a Mrs. Haze, whom he detests, and her twelve-year-old daughter Lolita, whom he would like to possess. He doesn't think of taking full possession of her, though Lolita is rather flirtatious with him. He has slyer and less perilous gratifications which result from her clowning intimacies with him. He marries Charlotte Haze, the mother, in order to be in a position to continue these intimacies with the daughter. But

Charlotte is hostile to her daughter and resents her presence and keeps planning to send her off to camp or school, or to transport herself and her husband to Europe. She wants to be alone with her "deep-voiced D.P." Humbert, who had not of course counted on these developments, would like to murder Charlotte. But he finds it more in keeping with his character to let events take care of themselves, which they quickly do. He has been careless about leaving his diary around; and Charlotte, exercising her wifely right to poke among his papers, finds and reads the diary and learns the truth. Lolita is Humbert's real love and Charlotte herself is only an "old cat." "You're a monster," she cries to him, with considerable justice. "You're a detestable, abominable, criminal fraud. If you come near—I'll scream out the window." But instead she rushes from the house, is hit by a passing car, and killed.

Humbert is now in possession of the Haze house, the Haze car, and—almost—the Haze girl. His neighbors kindly condole with him, married so recently, a stranger in a strange land, and with a wild stepdaughter on his hands. The son of the man whose car hit Charlotte arrives with a carefully executed diagram of the accident and a document waiving his father's responsibility for the death. Humbert obligingly signs the waiver and accepts the man's offer to pay the funeral expenses. He now proceeds to the seduction of Lolita, but again without the intention of *fully* seducing her. Taking her to a suburban hotel, where they register as father and daughter, he administers what he believes to be potent sleeping pills to Lolita in the hope of rendering her insensible to his furtive explorations. But the pills are placebos: Humbert's conscientious doctor has feared that he meant to attempt suicide in his grief; and in the end it is Lolita who completes the seduction of herself. It turns out that she has already been corrupted in her small girl way by a small boy at a summer camp.

She is Humbert's willing mistress this first night but soon reverts to her childish state and rebels when the intimacy threatens to become permanent. She has lost a bossy unloving mother only to acquire a too doting and despotic father. Humbert, insane with passion, makes a virtual prisoner of Lolita, bribing her with clothes and money and sundaes, and reminding her that if she should give him away to the authorites he would promptly be arrested and she would be detained for observation as a juvenile delinquent. They embark on a nightmarish journey by car across the United States. It is a wild flight from legality and reality. It is also a horribly inverted variant of a father and daughter tour, with stops at the best hostelries and visits to the historic sites and famous beauty spots.

There is a period during which Humbert seeks to keep Lolita by normalizing, as it were, their relationship. He installs her in a progressive school and settles himself nearby but is soon told by the unsuspecting school authorities that Lolita is emotionally in a bad way, needs more "home duties," and would profit by his relaxing his stern attitudes of an old-fashioned European father. Maybe, in fact, she should be analyzed. He takes alarm, and soon the strange pair are off again on their travels. This time, however, it soon appears that they are being pursued by a rival of Humbert's in a red convertible. The identity of his rival is unknown to Humbert but we presently learn that he is another middle-aged man, even more disreputable than Humbert, whom Lolita has met at the school and fallen in love with. The "transference" of the small girl's affections from her "father" to another and similar man has occurred. All very normal and on schedule.

The other man catches up with them at last and spirits Lolita away in an elaborate simulacrum of an elopement. Humbert the pursued becomes Humbert the pursuer and follows the pair from town to town, led on by a series of gloriously cryptic clues dropped by his comedian of a rival. This rival has the advantage over Humbert that he is a playwright of sorts, instead of being the mere fumbling impersonator that poor Humbert is. And Humbert, unable to decipher the clues and find the treasure, must finally give up the hunt. Several years pass, and then, in an amazing scene, he does find Lolita. Now seventeen, she is married to a kindly ex-GI who is hard of hearing. They are very poor and Lolita is pregnant—a conscientious wife, though still secretly in love with the playwright, who abandoned her. Once again Humbert bribes her, this time to learn the name of his original rival. Learning it, he sets out to perform the one fully meditated and willed act of his life. He kills the terrible man in a farcically protracted scene of violence in which the victim, though full of bullet holes, keeps bouncing back to life. How hard it is to destroy a man, how hard to eliminate so well-matched a rival!

Such a summary of the action naturally excludes most of the values that give subtlety to *Lolita* in the reading of it. These values mainly inhere in what Mr. Nabokov makes of Humbert Humbert. In the falsest of false positions, Humbert has enough decency to feel his position as what it is. He impersonates the hero of a novel, even though he isn't a hero by nature; and by some curious law he is more interesting as his actions become more outrageous. The prologue, recounting his early life, rings with a Frenchy sort of jocularity and is the least convincing part of *Lolita,* just as it is the most innocent part. The jocular tone of the prologue probably arises

from its being in some measure a burlesque of those Freudian flashbacks resorted to by many novelists in order to
make clear how the hero "got that way." However Humbert
got that way, we are made to see that he has become something which, in its grimness, quite defies explanation. It defies statistics, too, although his psychiatrist has informed him
that "at least 12% of American adult males—a 'conservative'
estimate according to Dr. Blanche Schwarzmann (verbal
communication)—enjoy yearly, in one way or another, the
special experience 'H.H.' describes with such despair." He is
the impossible sort of person whom Freud can't help, or Kin-
sey either: cocky, humorous, perceptive, fastidious, and almost too well read, too articulate ("You can always count on
a murderer for a fancy prose style"). His qualities are pretty
much at the command of his obsession, but he naturally
seeks to avoid the implications of his servitude and, like any
Vautrin or Raskolnikov, he plays his roles, assumes his
masks. Yet these impostures are not so much chosen by him
as thrust upon him by the conditions of his life; and brutally,
one after another, they are snatched away, exposing an awk-
ward grin. His very name lends itself to indiscriminate gar-
bling and tends to resolve itself into Humburg. He marries the
full-sized woman in Paris under the consoling impression
that he is irresistible to her (he thinks all adult women are
mad about him, and some are). But off she goes with a poor
specimen of a White Russian taxi driver and Humbert is left
with another interrupted relationship on his record, another
shattered mask at his feet.

With his entry upon the American scene his impersonations become more profound and his story takes on true stature. Indeed *Lolita* at this point begins to impersonate an
"international novel" (of the journalistic Graham Greene or

Koestler type rather than the Henry James type). The deep unreality within Humbert is complemented by another kind of unreality in the place of his destiny. He becomes subject to the preposterous chances and changes of a wide-open society, a culture madly on the move. His fate hangs on the godlike motions of the motorcar and the wayward oracle of the telephone. There is an ambiguous promise in the friendliness of small towns, the lush convenience of omnipresent hotels and motels, the defiant come-on of little girls in blue jeans, the suggestive innocence of the instruction they receive at school and the literature they read. " 'Mr. Uterus (I quote from a girls' magazine) starts to build a thick soft wall on the chance a possible baby may have to be bedded down there.' "

"It's a free country!" Lolita cries when her mother tries to send her to bed. Humbert is an ironic portrait of the visiting European, and the Hazes help to complete the likeness. He is to them the prince of a lost realm—actually a luxury hotel kept by his father on the Riviera. He seems to have the superior sexual acumen and appeal so often assumed by Europeans and envied by Americans—but his sexuality is as peculiar as we know. Mrs. Haze's husband, a hazy figure at best, has long been dead, and she and her daughter have made their pointless way from the Middle West to this New England town where Humbert arrives to be their boarder, ostensibly with the idea of writing a book in a peaceful retreat. The Haze women and their appurtenances are familiar enough; they have been portrayed in many satirical novels and problem plays of modern manners. There is the arty, career-bent, unloving mother; the defiant unloved daughter with her eternal blue jeans, her deplorable manners and secrets, her loud cries of "You dope!" and "I think you stink!";

and there is the litter of lamps, sofas, coffee tables, magazines, Van Gogh prints, and pink toilet-seat tidies amid which they irritably and insubstantially live. But the observations and machinations of Humbert, the sinister outsider, project a fierce glare on this trite house and its trite occupants, re-creating them and investing them with a sour pathos. "The poor lady [Charlotte Haze] was in her middle thirties, she had a shiny forehead, plucked eyebrows, and quite simple but not unattractive features of a type that may be defined as a weak solution of Marlene Dietrich . . . Her smile was but a quizzical jerk of one eyebrow; and uncoiling herself from the sofa as she talked, she kept making spasmodic dashes at three ash trays and the near fender (where lay the brown core of an apple); whereupon she would sink back again, one leg folded under her."

Charlotte Haze will soon uncoil herself for a more urgent reason and then dash impulsively into eternity. She is an ominous figure, a resonant type. With her "principles" which bulk large but weigh little, her vacuous animation, her habit of asserting herself although she has next to nothing in her to assert, Charlotte is the immoral moralist, the loveless romantic, the laughless comic—whatever it is that spoils the party and dampens the honeymoon all across America. Once married to Humbert she naturally imagines herself to be deeply attractive to him. She looms alluringly in slacks or bathing suit, coils and uncoils herself with more nervous abandon than ever, buys the pair of them a brand-new bed, cooks up fetching little messes for dinner, and in a frenzy of misplaced homemaking decides to redecorate the entire house. But her taste in these matters, which she owes to her culture, is no more attractive to Humbert than her robust femininity, for which nature is to blame. Her diluted Dietrich charms are lost on him, preoccupied as he is by the skinny charms of Lolita; but so would Dietrich at full strength be lost on him. Thus Charlotte is made to act out a timeless travesty of Woman, and of Sex itself with the rigid specializations and fetishisms that attend it in its capitalized form, or whenever it is an end in itself. Noting Humbert's gravitation towards Lolita and away from Charlotte, we can only wonder at the small affective range of *anyone's* desires. Why the one female rather than the other? Can a few years more or less, an inch or two of flesh at thigh or bosom, make *that* much difference? Then, as we learn, there is Humbert's rich distaste for fully developed co-eds—those much publicized love objects—and his horror at realizing that Lolita herself will soon be just another woman. ("I see, maybe, the coffin of coarse female flesh in which my nymphets are buried alive.") One man's meat is another man's mummy. Humbert is heir to the merry old European tradition of libertinage but he has forgotten the point of it. Rather, he has reduced it to absurdity and is himself reduced to all kinds of anxious fantasies and substitutive pleasures. Where the Marquis de Sade, that other specialized libertine, fed poisoned bonbons to his victims in the hope of seeing them writhe, Humbert avails himself of sleeping pills which only leave *his* victim thoroughly awake.

The scene at the Enchanted Hunters, the suburban hotel where Humbert and Lolita finally seduce one another, is one long spasm of comic horror—though now with a different drift from the Charlotte scenes—and Nabokov spares us nothing of Humbert's soft misery and dubious triumph. The famous scene in Proust in which Charlus pays to have himself flogged by personable young men who are only turning an honest penny in the interim of caring for their families and fighting for *la Patrie*—that scene appears heroically comic, almost like some adventure of Falstaff or Don Quixote, compared to the mean ironies that beat upon Humbert Humbert through the long night, while a religious convention is in progress in the hotel, and the corridors creak and the toilets groan familiarly, and Lolita refuses to give up her restless spirit to sleep.

Their historic night at the Enchanted Hunters is an initiation into the impostures and discomfitures of the motel-hopping life that awaits them. " 'The name,' I said coldly [to the room clerk], 'is not Humberg, and not Humbug, but Herbert, I mean Humbert, and any room will do, just put in a cot for my little daughter. She is ten and very tired.' " Humbert's guilty fears constantly stalk him. An inspector at the state line peers suspiciously into the car and says, "Any honey?" Tires go flat with an accusing plap-plap beneath them. All hostelries seem hostile, whether they are merely called the Kumfy Kabins or are elaborate affairs with notices on the wall that read:

We wish you to feel at home while here. All equipment was carefully checked upon your arrival. Your license number is on record here. Use hot water sparingly. We reserve the right to eject without notice any objectionable person. Do not throw waste material of ANY kind in the toilet bowl. Thank you. Call again. The Management. P.S. We consider our guests the Finest People in the World.

In the course of this insane journey, Humbert undergoes a reversal of roles and in so doing registers more and more sharply the real horror and the real significance of his partnership with Lolita. He first impersonated her father in order to elude the authorities, but in time he comes to feel more

and more like her actual father. Towards the end he begins
to reflect on the whole affair in the spirit of a parent who has
disappointed his child and been disappointed by her in turn.
"I often noticed that, living as we did, she and I, in a world of
total evil, we would become strangely embarrassed whenever I tried to discuss anything she and an older friend, she
and a parent, she and a real healthy sweetheart . . . might
have discussed . . . She would mail her invulnerability in
trite brashness and boredom, whereas I, using for my desperately detached comments an artificial tone of voice that set
my own last teeth on edge, provoked my audience to such
outbursts of rudeness as made any further conversation impossible, oh, my poor, bruised child."

Humbert's remorse is more effective for not clothing itself
in abstractly moral terms. He feels, not that he has betrayed
a "trust" of the kind that traditionally inheres in parenthood,
but that he has horribly let Lolita down as lover, friend, and
fellow human being, as well as in his capacity as father. The
consequence has been a complete sundering of human relations with her. Lolita herself, we learn at their last meeting,
has not been destroyed; indeed, she has exhibited the strange
capacity of the young to survive the worst abuses (other
things being equal). Nor is any forgiveness of him on her
part in question at this final meeting. Her career with him, so
painfully vivid in his own memory, has for her fallen into
place in a world of experience which she views as "just one
gag after another." If she originally called him Dad in bitter
irony, she now calls him Dad in sad earnest. But she doesn't
mean anything by it, any real affection, and it's too late anyway. His betrayal, not of a trust but of her, has done its work.
For of course he did betray her unspeakably. It did not constitute any justification of Humbert that she was his willing

mistress at first and already knew the ropes. On the contrary this only deepened and complicated his guilt. Outright rape would conceivably have counted for less than this queasy collusion, especially considering the orphaned state of Lolita, to whom he was after all her only excuse for a parent.

In all this, the distorting mirrors have been continuously at work, giving back a monstrous picture of what is again, like the grim sexual comedy of the Charlotte episode, a desperately common experience. The perverse partnership of Humbert and Lolita reflects some of the painful comedy of family relations in general. There is, on Lolita's side, the recurrent childhood feeling of being misunderstood, abused, betrayed by one's parents until at last—if one is lucky enough to grow up to that stage—one can accept them as part of the gag that life is, or even love them if one is luckier than Lolita. From Humbert's point of view, which is the predominating one, the situation is even more complicated, in fact, quite hopeless. He is the parent who sadly suspects that communication has broken down between himself and his child. Instead of conversation there is only a weary compulsive banter. Mutual trust is replaced by a shameful system of bargains and bribes: the "normal" man's form of collusion with his child. Desiring an affectionate and willing compliance with his wishes, he is fortunate if he can purchase a temporary docility with gifts of money, clothes, or chocolate sundaes. In his own eyes he becomes a mere purveyor of such material favors, and day after day he pays the too large bills at the endless motels of life. All the time, his suffering over the failure of love in his child is enhanced by his suspicion that it is all his fault. While trying to count up the blessings he has bestowed on her he remembers, as he fears that *she* remembers, only his acts of cruelty or indifference. He attempts now and then to repair the damage, restore communications. But he is quickly rebuffed in some unexpected way which confirms his original fears. " 'A penny for your thoughts,' I said, and she stretched out her palm at once." Those inaccessible thoughts, that outstretched palm! Such are the cares of a family man.

Considering the weird shapes of sexuality that *Lolita* assumes, the novel might appear to invite Freudian interpretations of the usual kind. Fathers want to sleep with their daughters, daughters with their fathers. The reverse of any such intention is the burden of *Lolita*. By parading the theme of incest, with drums and banners, Mr. Nabokov makes it ridicule itself out of existence so far as *Lolita* is concerned; and the same holds for the other evidences of popular Freudianism with which the tale is strewn. *Lolita*, far from being mythic, is anti-mythic in this respect. Mr. Nabokov cultivates the groans and guffaws of the recalcitrant fact, the embarrassment that yields to neither myth nor clinic, the bitter commonplaces of life's indestructible surface.

To say this, however, is to take *Lolita* at its best. The novel has its less than superlative moments, when the ribald fantastication gives way to a thin facetiousness or a pastiche of Joyce. In confessional novels of the intensity of *Lolita*, moreover, there is frequently a disquieting note of unresolved tension. It is present even in the great narratives of this character by Constant and Proust. The hero of such self-scrutinizing novels is both the culprit and the judge, an unlikely situation, and he must strain and strain to persuade us that he is at once bad enough to sin and good enough to repent. Humbert's "world of total evil" seems out of character, or at least in conflict with his idiom. It is the author intervening on Humbert's behalf and playing the role straight in order to make a vital point. So, too, with Humbert's belated love cries for his Lolita, which seem to be dictated by some principle of compensation and ring a little false (to me). "I was a pentapod monster, but I loved you. I was despicable and brutal and turpid, and everything, *mais je t'aimais, je t'aimais!" Lolita* is partly a masterpiece of grotesque comedy, partly an unsubdued wilderness where the wolf howls—a real wolf howling for a real Red Riding Hood.

1957

These remarks appeared in *The Anchor Review 2,* together with some excerpts from *Lolita,* which had not then been published in any form in America and did not seem likely ever to attain full publication here.

II. Nabokov: The Prose and Poetry of It All

Readers of *Lolita* may recall that Humbert Humbert, who delivers himself of the contents of the book while in confinement awaiting trial for murder, is something of a poet. "You can always count on a murderer for a fancy prose style," he says, and you can count on this particular murderer for scattered flights of verse as well. His are "occasional poems" in the most invidious sense possible. Humbert's muse materializes only intermittently, and when she does it is in response to situations of a kind that do not, as a rule, give rise to *la poésie pure*—or whatever we may call the opposite of occasional poetry.

Hoping, for example, to calm his restless Lolita he improvises a bit of what he tells her is "nonsense verse."

> The Squirl and his Squirrel, the Rabs and their Rabbits
> Have certain obscure and peculiar habits.
> Male humming birds make the most exquisite rockets.
> The snake when he walks holds his hands in his pockets.

"Nonsense is correct," Lolita says mockingly, perhaps guessing that Humbert's weakness for nymphets like herself lends the poem a certain "obscure and peculiar" sense which she would prefer to ignore. As a poet, Humbert succeeds no better with Rita, a temporary replacement for Lolita, and one who knows her time is short. He tries to stop her accusing sobs by extemporizing some verses about a certain "blue hotel" they have just motored past. "Why blue when it is white, why blue for heaven's sake?" she protests and starts crying again. Humbert's lengthiest effort is a ballad, full of literary allusions, *double-entendres*, and straight French, which he writes to console himself for the loss of Lolita. One stanza reads:

> Happy, happy is gnarled McFate
> Touring the States with a child wife,
> Plowing his Molly in every State
> Among the protected wild life.

Humbert, like other of Nabokov's creatures, foreign or nutty or both, has a peculiar flair for knowing what is going on in the American literary world. He knows, for example, that "light verse" has been made respectable by Mr. W. H. Auden, whose own fine efforts in that form have rarely excelled Humbert's McFate ballad. He knows, too, that poetry of *any* weight lends itself nicely to depth analysis. His own analyst, Humbert says of his ballad: "It is really a maniac's masterpiece. The stark, stiff, lurid rhymes correspond very exactly to certain perspectiveless and terrible landscapes and figures . . . as drawn by psychopaths in tests devised by astute trainers." He is aware, too, of that specialty of American poetics, the belief that poetry inheres in phenomena themselves rather than in the poet and that to compose a poem one need only catalogue phenomena in sufficiently impressive numbers. So he pounces upon a mimeographed list of the names of Lolita's classmates, surnames and first names intriguingly reversed for the purpose of alphabetization (e.g., FANTAZIA, STELLA; FLASHMAN, IRVING; HAZE, DOLORES). "A poem, a poem, forsooth!" he exclaims, and goes on to imagine the occupants of the classroom: "Adorable Stella, who has let strangers touch her; Irving, for whom I am sorry, etc." Nor does Humbert's muse desert him on the ultimate occasion. When, gun in hand, he delivers sentence on his rival Clare Quilty prior to shooting him dead, he does so in the accents of a certain poem, well known to the literary world, about sin, penitence, and death:

> Because you took advantage of a sinner
> because you took advantage
> because you took
> because you took advantage of my disadvantage . . .

"That's damned good," says Quilty, providing Humbert with an approving, if captive, audience at last.

For Humbert, the uses of poetry are rather low. He might even be said to prostitute his muse. The uses of poetry for Mr. Nabokov are high, though not so high as to rule out the efforts of those who are compelled into song by mixed motives, including lust, revenge, and the hope of a check from *The New Yorker*. Like that other master of prose, James Joyce, Mr. Nabokov aspired in youth to be a poet. More than Joyce did, he has continued to write verse and to fill his novels with reflections on poetry. The reflections are often of major importance; the verse—the verse in English at least—is minor, as minor as verse could be and still remain interesting. His forthcoming translation of Pushkin's *Eugene Onegin* will conceivably stand as his main poetic achievement. For years he has been going on about Pushkin ("the gold reserve of our literature"), meanwhile preparing us for the *magnum opus* by translating other Russian poets. He brings to poetry and the informal criticism of poetry the same spirit of connoisseurship that enlivens his work as a whole—an impassioned connoisseurship that unites the naturalist in him with the literary artist in him and does duty, it would seem, for ideology. He has a mind too rich to be impoverished by ideas. His "commitment" (in the starkly fashionable sense) is to perceptions, discriminations, prejudices, and to the purveying, as he says, of "aesthetic bliss." Before 1940, when he came to live in the United States and started publishing in English, he contributed a number of poems to Russian *émigré* periodicals in Europe. Between 1943 and 1957 he wrote the fourteen poems which, described as "his complete poetic works in English," were collected in a miniature volume succinctly entitled *Poems* (1959). *Pale Fire*, his most recent novel in English (1962), consists of a long poem, or quasi-poem, ostensibly written by an American poet, and of lengthy notes ostensibly supplied by a European-born editor.

The last novel Mr. Nabokov wrote in Russian has lately come out in English—authentic Nabokovian English. *The Gift* is a delightful novel. It is also invaluable for what it tells us about its author's relation to the twin disciplines of poetry and prose, in the past as, I venture, at present. With *The Gift* as a main text, let me inquire into those relations, to the extent that I can do so in short space and with no knowledge of Russian.

The Gift has been widely and pleasantly reviewed during the months since it appeared. So far as I am aware, however, no one has pointed out that the book is a sort of hail and farewell to the poetic muse considered as a full-time companion. A young poet formidably named Fyodor Godunov-Cherdyntsev is the hero. (One of *The Gift*'s best reviewers, Mr. Stanley Edgar Hyman, tells us this was Nabokov's own pen name as a poet—he signed his novels V. Sirin.) An *émigré* Russian who has forfeited much to the Bolsheviks—a country estate, a St. Petersburg town house, probably a father, possibly a future as a native writer, Fyodor lives an exile's desultory life in Berlin. There he moves from furnished room to furnished room, gives stupid Germans reluctant Russian lessons, composes verses, imagines the fine reviews his recently published book of poems will get, recalls his Russian childhood, mingles diffidently with his quarrelsome fellow exiles, loses his keys, gets his clothes stolen at the Grünewald swimming lake. His life is almost as unreal as the phenomenon we find him scrutinizing on the novel's first page: a moving van with "the name of the moving company in yard-high blue letters, each of which (including a square dot) was shaded laterally with black paint—a dishonest attempt to climb into the next dimension." Fyodor seeks to climb into the next dimension, the heaven of aesthetic bliss, by the frail but not dishonest ladder of poetry alone. True, he has a distinct "gift" for it, a charming craze for words, and a capacity for hallucination that verges on secular mysticism. The first chapter of *The Gift* is, among other things, a little anthology of his poems. They are about incidents remembered from his childhood in Russia.

My ball has rolled under Nurse's commode.
On the floor a candle
Tugs at the ends of the shadows
This way and that, but the ball is gone . . .

Knocked from its hiding place by a poker, the ball *"Crosses the whole room and promptly goes under/The impregnable sofa."* The long line nicely reproduces the effect of the ball's trip across the room. And the ball stays lost.

As the novel unfolds, we see Fyodor's situation—which resembles the ball's—reflected back at him in various ways by the plight of other *émigrés* around him in Berlin. There is the tragedy (or tragic farce) of the young poet Yasha, a recent suicide, whose hopeless attachment to a German youth of the blond and blue-eyed type forms, incidentally, a grim parody of a familiar Thomas Mann theme. There is the pure farce of Mr. Busch, a Latvian with pretensions to poetic drama. Before an audience choking with stifled laughter, he reads his "new, philosophical tragedy." It is *Faust* out of *Brand* out of Busch, and includes the following conversation in a "Street of Sin":

> FIRST PROSTITUTE
> All is water. That is what my client Phales* says.
> SECOND PROSTITUTE
> All is air, young Anaximines told me.
> THIRD PROSTITUTE
> All is number. My bald Pythagoras cannot be wrong.
> FOURTH PROSTITUTE
> Heracles* caresses me whispering "All is fire."
> LONE COMPANION (enters)
> All is fate.

"There is no great poetry without parody," Fyodor explains; and in *The Gift* the parodies tend to be better than the poems. So Fyodor begins to feel that he will eventually want "to speak in quite another way, not in miniature verse

---

* It is Busch's fault, not the proofreader's, that Thales becomes Phales, Anaximenes becomes Anaximines, and Heraclitus becomes Heracles. [F.W.D.]

with charms and chimes, but in very, very different manly words." Indeed, during an imaginary conversation with an older poet he respects, Fyodor hears the man say: "By the way, I've read your very remarkable volume of poems. Actually, of course, they are but models of your future novels." Fyodor then stops trying to recapture his childhood. Instead, he undertakes to reconstruct, first the final days of his beloved father, a celebrated naturalist who has vanished on a scientific expedition to Asia, the victim of an accident or of the Bolsheviks; second, the life of Chernyshevski, the celebrated social critic of the 1860's, father of Russian utlilitarianism, Lenin's mentor. For these projects, Fyodor abandons verse, wooing instead "the Muse of Russian prose-rhythms." His assault on Chernyshevski's crude version of the liberal imagination strangely foreshadows the assault that Proust, at the start of *his* career as a serious writer, made for somewhat similar reasons on Sainte-Beuve. But *Contre Sainte-Beuve* (which, incidentally, is of recent discovery and could not therefore have been in Mr. Nabokov's mind during the years 1935-37 when *The Gift* was written) is the tirade of a tyro compared to Nabokov-Fyodor's explosive yet touching portrait of Chernyshevski, whose dreadful sufferings as a man effectively belied his doctrinaire optimism as a philosopher. Rejected by a publisher as "a syringe of sulphuric acid," the Chernyshevski portrait is really part of Fyodor's attempt to contemplate Russian history without nostalgia—that nostalgia of the exile which, in Nabokov's view, so often ends in the exile's paranoia. "Why," he asks, "had everything in Russia become so shoddy, so crabbed and gray, how could she have become so befooled and befuddled? Or had the old 'urge toward the light' concealed a fatal flaw, which in the course of progress toward the objective had grown more and

more evident, until it was revealed that this 'light' was burning in the window of a prison overseer, and that was all?"

But Fyodor's attempt to climb into the next dimension depends on other things than writing. He must unite himself,
with a pretty, intelligent, hard-working girl who loves him
and his poems, her name being Zina Mertz. Zina embodies,
along with a poetic sensibility, the advantages—figuratively
speaking—of good prose. Is this putting it too neatly? I think
not. The novel itself has a rather pat way of making its
points, a somewhat mechanical way of contriving its games
of reality and appearance. After all, *The Gift* is a comparatively early work. In most respects, though, the mature
Nabokov is already in command. Fyodor and Zina meet in a
setting that is prosaic with a vengeance. It is one of those
superlatively dreary interiors, epitomized by the communal
bathroom and the communal bar of soap with the single hair
in it, which Nabokov loves to swoop down on, whether in
Berlin or the U.S.A., from the high wire of fantasy. This feeling for the commonplace at its commonest shows that his
affinity with Joyce equals his affinity (more obvious in *The
Gift*) with Proust. Fyodor writes a poem addressed to Zina
but printed as prose. "Look at that street—it runs to China
straight, and yonder star above the Volga glows!" Thus, in a
fashion, the man and the woman, the exile and his homeland,
the poet and the prose writer are all momentarily united.

Need we conclude that Mr. Nabokov himself has "sacri-
ficed" poetry to prose? I doubt it. The English poems, all but
two of them first printed in *The New Yorker*, are, it is true, of
a kind often called, with a certain condescension, "lapidary."
Nevertheless, as Mr. Nathaniel Reicheck has suggested, "the
poet goes beyond the limits of his art [the "light verse" art]
without violating its canon. This enlargement of a traditional

form is made possible by his campaign to re-design the English language. His prosody is a unique and subtle parody of the original." This, again, may be overstating things, but not by much. The English poems do have a peculiar miniature excellence: perfect lucidity, precise wit, the glow of a lighted candle cupped in an expert hand against the windy verse roundabout. "A Literary Dinner" turns on a misunderstanding such as might occur between an American hostess whose enunciation was unclear and a foreign guest whose ear was imperfectly tuned to slurred English. "I want you, she murmured, to eat Dr. James." And so, amid dull talk at the table, he does eat Dr. James.

> All was good and well-cooked, but the tastiest part
> was his nut-flavored, crisp cerebellum. The heart
> resembled a shiny brown date,
> and I stowed all his studs on the edge of my plate.

Such a *nice* foreign guest, obliging, hungry, and neat. For wit mingled with lyrical delight, "An Evening of Russian Poetry" comes closest to being "great"—besides being a helpful treatise on versification. Referring to the Russian poets' "passion for expansion," the lecturer goes on to exemplify it in several asides, by turns paranoiac and nostalgic in mood.

> My back is Argus-eyed. I live in danger.
> False shadows turn to track me as I pass . . .

> Beyond the seas where I have lost a sceptre
> I hear the neighing of my dappled nouns,
> soft participles coming down the steps,
> treading on leaves, trailing their rustling gowns,
> and liquid verbs in *ahla* and in *ili,*
> Aonian grottoes, nights in the Altai,
> black pools of sound with 'L's' for water lilies.

The empty glass I touched is tinkling still,
but now 'tis covered by a hand and dies . . .

While writing his English verses Nabokov was elaborating the English prose which, somewhat subdued in *Sebastian Knight,* sometimes out of hand in *Bend Sinister,* would culminate in the controlled sinuosities of *Lolita,* the almost paranoid eloquence of *Pale Fire.* Kinbote's eloquence, I mean, for the point of the novel, rhetorically speaking, seems to lie in the contrast between the inflamed yet often beautiful writing of Kinbote's editorial notes and the paler fires, the intermittent beauties, of John Shade's poem. Mary McCarthy has said much about the book in her superb analysis and panegyric in *The New Republic.* One need only add a few words on Shade's poem itself. Distressed by his daughter's suicide, the father tries to convey his grief, his thoughts on death in general, in a kind of Popian four-part epistle constructed of the appropriate couplets. But he cannot rise either to Pope's scarifying realism or to the dashing architectonics of Pope's verse. Shade starts to quote the great lines from the *Essay on Man:*

See the blind beggar dance, the cripple sing,
The sot a hero, lunatic a king.

But he breaks the lines midway, explaining that "they smack of their heartless age." Shade's poem has an inner subject that goes unperceived by either Shade or his editor, who imagines the poem is about him and *his* "lost sceptre," *his* living "in danger." The inner subject is the blindness of Shade's grief, his helplessness before the extremities of passion and death, the spiritual deformity which was his daughter's sole inheritance from him but which the singing cripple of Pope's lines and the crippled Pope himself do not share. So the poem maunders along, lovely in spots, penetrating in other spots, now elegiac, now cheery. It clothes itself in a simulacrum of Popian couplets without attaining to the hard antitheses, the decisive pauses, which are the prosodic mirror of Pope's tougher mind.

John Shade is a kindly, even affectionate, portrait of the American poet-in-residence. Like Robert Frost he maintains a stoic patience and a well-ordered life in the face of domestic disaster. As with lesser specimens of the type his muse is so thoroughly "in residence," so domesticated, that he is impelled, on one hand into academic verse, on the other into drink. Indeed, he could do with some of Kinbote's madness and passion, just as Kinbote could do with a lot of Shade's common sense. But the exchange of qualities does not take place. Instead, Shade gets the bullet intended for Kinbote—or, more accurately, for Kinbote's landlord. In *Pale Fire*, as so often in our author's work, it takes two men to make a proper Nabokovian man—two men who, however, rarely succeed in uniting. With a writer, if he is a genius, the duality may be made to work for him, just as the Siamese twins in the story, "Scenes from the Life of a Double Monster," are finally put to work by Uncle Novus. Nabokov has done the same with the poet and novelist in him, made of them a team. Thus he has been able to perfect an English prose medium whose flexibility is adapted to the astonishing range, the endless contradictions, of his nature, of Nature itself. Some of those future novels of which Fyodor's poems were the models have, we know, already come into being. After the translation of Pushkin's novel in verse, others may follow.

1963

Libido
is a Latin
Word

Thanks to the University of Michigan Press, the scandalous old *Satyricon* of Petronius now circulates freely in a candid translation at moderate cost. Mr. Arrowsmith is explicit where former translators recoiled prudently into the original Latin or into coy English double talk. He also tries to foster, by his choice of an idiom, the "illusion," as he calls it in his introduction, "of contemporaneity." The idiom is not his own idiom as a writer but, as he explains, is composed of a selection from current American speech and literary prose. Thus it is a frankly experimental, not to say artificial, idiom and in practice it has the limitations you might expect from such a creation. Expressions such as "cheap bastard," "for kicks," "just peanuts," and "running around like crazy" appear frequently, and they seem not to consort well either with each other or with the passages of more standard prose. Unlike Ezra Pound in his adaptations from the Latin of Propertius, Mr. Arrowsmith does not, as a rule, succeed in fostering the illusion of contemporaneity.

With that, however, I reach the end of my complaints. The Latin of *The Satyricon* is even more complicated than Propertius's Latin. Now racy, now formal, charged with sudden ironies, tending always to parody, and strewn with poems in various meters and styles, it has been a problem to translators at all periods. Mr. Arrowsmith renders the poems exceedingly well; each is a true *tour de force*. And if his prose tends to sound artificial in the very act of trying to sound natural, it has great advantages over the fake Elizabethanese of J. M. Mitchell, author of a popular rendering of *The Satyricon* in the old Broadway Translations series. Based, moreover, on the latest editions of a much abused and emended text, the Arrowsmith rendering is trustworthy, clear, easy to follow, and, as I said, explicit. Here, then, is the inflammatory *Satyricon* in a form that all may read. The democratization of culture and the liberation of sex could go no further.

For the book belongs, of course, to literary culture as well as to that interesting department of writing called "erotica" and thus has a double claim on our attention at present. T. S. Eliot's complaint, in the erotica-loving 1920's, that *The Satyricon* seemed to be the one work of classical literature universally known to modern readers, no longer applies. The combined efforts of the Great Books advocates and our intrepid poet-scholar-translators have restored much of classical literature to the schoolroom and the bookshelf. A consciousness of ancient myth and drama now broods over current literature and criticism and sometimes appears to haunt them. If Arrowsmith's *Satyricon* follows in *Lolita*'s wake, it also forms an item in a series of "Classics in Translation" issued by the same university press and led off by the morally impeccable Hesiod. A modern rendering of *The Satyricon* was in order and has been needed. Long a prize puzzle to scholars and a mighty challenge to moralists, the book has also been an inspiration to writers from Voltaire and Flaubert to Gide, Joyce, Fitzgerald, and Eliot himself. A passage from *The Satyricon*, about the caged sybil who wants only to die, forms the epigraph of *The Waste Land;* and both works are filled with the shapes of impotence and death. Yet the differences between the two are, to say the least, striking. The one is as implacably tragic and Christian as the other is implacably comic and pagan.

Nothing, however, can really be said about the work's meanings until some account has been given of the mysteries and problems that have accumulated around the text. Like its hero, the luckless but indomitable Encolpius, *The Satyricon* has had a fugitive career in time and space, coming down to us in a sadly mutilated form, and with no fully accredited author or date of composition to lend it historical respectability. When, where, and by whom was this improbable farrago of sex and sensibility conceived? What went on in the infinitely receding distances of a story that seems to begin, as it certainly ends, in the air? What, for that matter, went on during those lapses of continuity—grimly called lacunae by scholars—that are always making the scene go dark in the surviving sections? Was the book ever really completed or did the author's creative purpose, like the amorous purpose of Encolpius himself, flag at the climactic moment? Whatever its original form was, why are there no known allusions to *The Satyricon* among ancient writings?

Questions of date and authorship are settled with one stroke if one accepts, as many classicists including Mr. Arrowsmith now do, the tradition that Petronius Arbiter, Nero's sometime courtier and ultimate victim, wrote *The Satyricon* during the latter half of the first century A.D. A distinguished modern scholar, Mr. Gilbert Highet, goes on to claim that *The Satyricon* was composed by Petronius with the idea of treating Nero to a vicarious slumming trip through the lower depths and outer fringes of Roman society. Others tend to doubt—on principle, since facts are lacking—that a book of this highly original character could have been written by any mere courtier of this world, ancient or modern. On the contrary, the author might well have been some provincial of genius, on the order if not the scale of Shakespeare and Joyce. Besides, the evidence of history (Tacitus and Suetonius) suggests that Nero was not shy about slumming on his own.

The novelty of *The Satyricon* is generally acknowledged by classicists even while they struggle to supply the book with a prominent author and to fit it into one or another of the established genres of Roman literature. The author's originality, and his consciousness of it, appear in the uncommon energy of his language, the boldness of his comic inventions, and the uncompromising thought implicit in his story. Using the first person, itself a rare practice in classical narrative, he makes it pay off in his feats of characterization and specialized speech. The traditional device of mistaken or disguised identities here takes on new dimensions.

Encolpius, the narrator, has a number of roles but is thrown among people who mostly play their own roles more successfully than he plays his. A knight among rich and powerful freedmen, a poor tutor among established teachers of rhetoric, a part-time con man among more skilled practitioners of the game, a sincere lover among unscrupulous libertines, he is above all a mere man living among the shadows and memories of the more heroic males of epic and romance. Like Odysseus, he has offended deity and been obliged to suffer for it through long wanderings. But the deity Encolpius offended is not any Olympian, only the half-serious lust god Priapus; and Encolpius' sufferings consist in his being set upon—most unheroically—by lustful females and eunuchs, doused with aphrodisiacs, shaved of his hair, fitted out in women's wigs, tumbled in fishponds.

In short, Encolpius seems to embody one of those back-handed tributes to common humanity which—as in the case of Mr. Bloom of *Ulysses*—are ridden with ironic contradictions. On the one hand Encolpius is only what Mr. Arrowsmith says his name implies, "the Crotch," a poor, bare, forked animal. On the other hand he is gallant, charming, idealistic, and indomitable: our own man, however absurd.

Encolpius' adventures generally involve sexual experiences of the most flagrant kind. *Libido,* a word that occurs in the Latin text, is more than a life force animating all the characters. It suggests a live wire with which they have all come into galvanizing contact. They enter on sexual relations as readily as we shake hands with an acquaintance. Just as no one is reproved except out of jealousy, so there are no innocents and no common "norms" to govern the choice of a sexual partner. In the gay unformulated pragmatism of this world anything goes if it works; one takes one's "love object" where one finds it, in persons of either sex or any age. And it is no dream, no projection of the unconscious such as gives a basis in psychological realism to the Night Town scenes in *Ulysses* and other examples of modern literary fantasy. What happens in *The Satyricon* happens in the clearest of Mediterranean lights to people who may be, as it were, electrified, but who are wide awake and in their right minds.

Mr. Arrowsmith theorizes about all this promiscuity in a way that may make the book more acceptable to modern readers but that seems to me to distort its meaning, besides receiving no support that I can discover from the text. As in

Lolita, he says, we here view the world's disorder through
the eyes of a still more disordered individual, through "the
prejudiced eyes of a first-person pederast" (Encolpius); "in
this way the mocker is mocked in return, his pretensions exposed in his own rhetorical passion, and his cool raffish eye
clouded by what he cannot see: his own absurdity." But isn't
Encolpius absurd, as I have suggested, because he is "human" and not because of his love affairs alone? How, moreover, does his pederasty differ from that of the other characters? And how does his "rhetorical passion" differ from the
rhetorical passion indulged in by most of them in one way
or another?

All eyes are "prejudiced" here. The divorce between sensibility and actuality is a constant theme of the book. In particular, a comic exaltation of sexual actuality unites with the
ironic exaltation of common humanity in Encolpius and
others. All this makes *The Satyricon* at once relevant and irrelevant to an age like ours—an age divided at the top between philosophical sensualists and philosophical ascetics,
Lawrences and Eliots, all of them intent on rationalizing, pro
or con, something that in itself resists such efforts, namely
sex. As Mr. Gore Vidal has remarked, "Sex *is.*"

To the sensualist, the book makes its appeal solely through
the frankness of its sexual scenes. But these are rarely idyllic,
and even then they are subject to rude interruptions. Orgies
become roughhouses, dealing out pain and humiliation,
though of a slapstick kind. Expurgate these images rather
thoroughly and you have the hurly-burly of an early Chaplin
film. In the author's unrelenting comic view, sex is as supremely funny as it is ineradicably "human."

"Wholesome" is Mr. Arrowsmith's oddly chosen word for

The Satyricon's impact on the ethical constitution of readers. He claims that it is not only "moral," in the cant of our time, but positively good for you. And in an odd way, he may be right.

1960

In the
Powers
Country

J. F. Powers has long enjoyed an inconspicuous fame as the author of two volumes of short stories, *The Prince of Darkness* and *The Presence of Grace*. These volumes, together with his recently published novel, *Morte d'Urban*, make up Powers's entire work. The outcome of twenty years of writing, the work is obviously not extensive but it is very good. And *Morte d'Urban*, a comic novel of great charm and point, casts its glow back over the short stories, of which it seems the inevitable extension.

Mr. Powers's work is all the more interesting because its prime subject is one that has been little exploited by American writers and that would seem, in fact, to hold little promise for them. His subject is the contradictions that beset Catholicism, in practice if not in theory, because of its claim to an earthly as well as a divine mission and authority. Powers is, however, a very down to earth, very American, Catholic. In his work, the contradictions are expressed, not in any of those flagrant dramas of sin and redemption which form the staples of Christian romance, but in the simple spectacle of priests going about the ordinary business of their professions. From this spectacle, however, he evokes a mingling of severity and raillery that is not simple. It seems to have confused several reviewers of *Morte d'Urban*, even one as intelligent as Stanley Edgar Hyman, who wrote: "It is very funny when Father Urban . . . is wet on by a hamster but it is not the Dark Night of the Soul." Definitely not, and J. F. Powers is not Graham Greene, with whom Mr. Hyman rather unfortunately compared him. In the soul, as we glimpse it in Powers's stories, it is not always three o'clock in the morning; it practically never is. By stating his objections to *Morte d'Urban,* however, Mr. Hyman indirectly defined the grounds of Powers's special excellence. In his own way he is a thorough realist, even a regionalist. His explorations into novelistic reality are confined to a locale that is small enough and distinct enough to be knowable in terms of what he wants to know about it. Improbably, for a writer of his faith, his locale is traditionally Lutheran Minnesota. The advantage to him of this setting, however, is just that it intensifies the essential contradictions. His fictive Minnesota is a country of interminable flats, vague lakes and woodlands, and slightly hostile natives. It is very far from Rome (traditional Rome) and centuries away from St. John of the Cross. The distance lends a certain unreality to Church Latin, black habits, medieval vows, and dogmatic assumptions; and from this unreality arises some of the severity and much of the hilarity of the whole spectacle of priestly endeavor in Powers's domain. Yet neither the vague unrealities nor the all too raw realities of his Minnesota keep Powers from depicting it with restrained affection: the heart has, apparently, its regions. Nor are his ecclesiatics and their lay followers submitted to the kind of doctrinaire scrutiny which might see them as all of a piece. True, Powers excels at portraying specimens of "the terrible thing a false vocation can be"—irate beer-swilling Fathers whose inner wastelands make a desolation all around them.

But there is always somewhere, portrayed with the same skill, belonging to the same novelistic world, some austerely dedicated cleric to judge the falsifiers. And there is the old Franciscan, Father Didymus, of "Lions, Harts, Leaping Does," who seems to attain authentic holiness, if only when he is at the point of death.

Death, however, is a rare thing in Powers's world, and so is any theological obsession with mortality in general. His characters, both lay and ecclesiastic, are remarkable for their stubborn grasp on life, their fierce little wills, their flat assertive speech, their aggressive actions. They make vivid characters for fiction but have too much character for the good of their souls. And the mortuary solution is withheld from them as, possibly, too easy.

Powers's is a world of the living all too living, and only in such a world can the ethical consideration bear much weight. For the purposes of fiction, he effects a divorce between faith and morals. The question is not whether faith, in the measure his characters have it, makes them greatly better or greatly worse than those outside the fold. The question is whether those inside the fold can sustain the moral life at the level of *average* good will, self-respect and taste. If this approach is necessary to Powers as a moral realist, it is also congenial to him as a storyteller; and his love of narration in all shapes, sizes and degrees of seriousness is obvious. Stories within stories, ranging from rectory-table anecdotes through biblical parables to scraps of radio serials caught from the airwaves, thicken the fictional atmosphere. Each sentence tends to be an event; yet every event, like every firm but fluent sentence, is an open door into the next half-expected, half-shocking encounter. Thus does J. F. Powers coax stories out of the shabby rectories of his not altogether mythical Minnesota.

Morte d'Urban is his supreme fiction so far and its hero, Father Urban, is his largest and gayest embodiment of the old contradiction. "You may be right," is Father Urban's slogan, his favorite formula of moral accommodation. Another Sir Lancelot, brave, beautiful and gracious, he has a weakness for his worldly Guinevere, which in Father Urban's case is several aggressive laymen (and lay-women) headed by an especially alluring and awful Chicago tycoon. (I suspect that the Malory echoes are meant to provide only grace notes to the comic tune of the novel: isn't just about every modern fictional hero required to establish an "ironic" relation with some figure out of mythology?) Actually, Father Urban's too accommodating spirit springs from a certain quality of radiant good will about him, a quality which, far from being evil in itself, is ideally human and generically "American." If the chances of an impoverished childhood had not made a priest of him, Father Urban would be imaginable as a vastly superior Babbitt, a Gatsby whose romance with life is better rewarded than Gatsby's was, an Eisenhower whose golf, like his English, is more expert than that of the recent President. Even as a priest Father Urban keeps his radiance until the temptations of "Guinevere" combine with the envy of his fellow ecclesiastics to bring out the contradiction. Then, to be sure, he gets his come-uppance, in a crescendo of "ordeals" or "trials" as touching as they are ludicrous. Yet, as a reviewer in *The Commonweal* pointed out, these culminate, not in the actual "morte" of the hero but in the demise, so to speak, of his worldliness, an event that apparently makes possible, though it doesn't guarantee, his redemption.

Meanwhile Father Urban, though without a developed spiritual vocation, has a healthy respect for the priesthood considered as a *profession*. As such his role is very dear to him, and he plays it throughout with charm and tact. It is true that his performance during the "ordeals" or "trials" is not in its moral essence superior to that of any self-respecting man belonging to a respected profession. Such a man could be trusted to object, as Father Urban objects, when a brutal hunter tries to drown a helpless deer. Such a man could perhaps even be trusted to resist, as Father Urban does, the drunken provocations of the woman who, in very ominous circumstances, throws off her clothes and invites him to join her in a midnight swim. For the question, again, is one of *average* standards of decency. Yet few men could hope to come through it all with the fine masculine *élan* that Father Urban shows and that makes him such a marvelous literary creation. His fellow priests avoid such scrapes, not because they have the grace of God in them, but because they are merely less enterprising or more prudent than he is.

Father Urban is the central figure in what is—if such labels apply here—a comedy with strong satirical overtones. The point is distinctly made that, according to *Time* magazine, the Catholic Church is second only to Standard Oil among American corporate enterprises. And the satire shows, among other things, to what an extent *Time*'s claim is literally true. The satire shows the earthly church in its guise as an immense if rather antiquated corporate enterprise, its priests mostly job-holders, its upper hierarchy an arbitrary and oppressive bureaucracy. Father Urban's troubles begin when, all too successful as a churchly go-getter in Chicago, he is banished by his jealous Father Provincial to a decrepit mansion on the Minnesota plains which his decrepit order has acquired by gift and which it hopes to convert into a prosperous home for retreatants. Here Father Urban is obliged to labor as a common workman under the command of obscure Father Wilfrid, an excruciatingly comic figure of militant mediocrity. And here, too, *Morte d'Urban* begins clearly to show its hand—or both its hands—and to take on the character of an ecclesiastical satire which is also a satire of American culture. The forlorn circle of clerics at work on the retreat are, from another point of view, just a bunch of fellows on their uppers trying to patch up an old hotel into a paying proposition, buying their supplies from a discount house, getting out cheap brochures, and arousing the suspicions of the natives. And so on, throughout the main body of the narrative—which has been criticized as "episodic" but which is just lucid and well-timed far beyond the average. Successively, Father Urban is juxtaposed to many well-known features of the American cultural scene. One by one, the golf match, the drag race, the McCarthyite journal, the wild party, the dreary lakeside cottage, the dreary lunchroom meal, the TV set, the electrified crèche, insinuate themselves into his destiny. Sustained by Powers's gift for discreetly daring invention, the effect is satire at its most amusing and deadly. Gazing down from a church on a new housing development "whose windows, yards and rooftops were all lit up for Christmas," an elegant Monsignor mutters: "The fires of hell, and in the summertime, with all those barbecue pits going, it smells like Afghanistan." The American Church, caught in its contradictions, is not far from suggesting the same fires and smells, even though the finely managed transition to a more sober conclusion shows, I suppose, the author's essential piety, his eternally springing hope.

As with some thickly peopled and richly developed small country, the size of Powers's work is relative to the delight one feels on discovering it and immersing oneself in its particulars. My own delight in doing so has been great.

1963

Malamud:
The Uses and
Abuses of
Commitment

Looking up Malamud in Leslie Fiedler's capacious *Love and Death in the American Novel* I find that the treatment of him there is surprisingly brief and unenthusiastic. Given Mr. Fiedler's well-known prepossessions I should have expected him to award Malamud high marks. Fiedler is carrying the torch for "mature genital sexuality"—something that he finds deplorably lacking in the erotic life of the American novel. I have myself just read, not only the recent *Idiots First,* but all of Mr. Malamud's work that I can find in print; and it is my impression that the sexual norm of his world is eminently normal, as in fact it would have to be since his people are mostly too busy establishing themselves and their families in an elementally hostile world to feel desire in excessive or distorted forms.

True, they often suffer mildly from an *insufficiency* of sexual fulfillment, especially when they are young. But this suffering is apt to seek relief in the simpler forms of action, namely in going to bed with the opposite sex, or trying to. At worst, the deprivation manifests itself in a sexual curiosity so candid as scarcely to deserve the fancy term "voyeurism." In no other author, surely, are so many pretty girls so sweetly obliging about getting undressed in front of their boy friends. "Would you mind if I peeled and went in for a dip?"

the girl student asks her teacher in "A Choice of Profession," a story in *Idiots First*. "Go ahead," the teacher says happily, and she does. But "A Choice of Profession" is not, as this scene by itself might suggest, one of those steamy romances with a campus setting. The student turns out to have been a call girl in her past life; and the teacher, on her telling him this, recoils from her in fear and disgust even though he is so far from being a lily himself that he has been entertaining furtive designs on her. But he is only a prig, not a creep; and the point as finally voiced by him is that "It's hard to be moral."

In Malamud's novel, *The Assistant,* to be sure, we have in the Italian youth, Frank Alpine, a bad case of distorted sexuality. He is a thief, a peeping Tom and, just once, a rapist. But Frank is by definition an outsider, especially in the Jewish family that shelters him. Even so, he finally atones for everything. He settles down, marries the girl he raped, has himself circumcized and becomes a Jew. The lesson is as clear as the lesson is in *The Golden Bowl,* where James's Anglo-Saxon girl succeeds in reforming *her* beloved Italian, the adulterous Prince Amerigo. Essentially the lesson is the same in both authors. Mature sexuality culminating in marriage is the norm. And so potent a force is the norm that it accomplishes not only the regeneration of the erring ones but their actual or virtual assimilation to another culture. Indeed "assimilation," but with the Jew seeking the moral assimilation of the non-Jew, is a basic principle of Malamud's work. And as concerns sex, the power of the Jew is reinforced by his relative normality.

If Mr. Fiedler fails to credit Malamud with his own sexual values it is because he has other tests that Malamud's work fails to pass. Fiedler is carrying a second torch: for the

"Gothic" strain in American fiction. Gothic fantasy, he believes, "provides a way into not only the magic world of the baseball fan . . . but also into certain areas of our social life where nightmare violence and guilt actually exist." The reference here is to Malamud's first novel, *The Natural*, which is about the heroics and horrors of professional baseball. Influenced, apparently, by Nathanael West's mordant dealings with American folklore, *The Natural*, true to its Westian prototypes, explodes at one point into bloody fantasy. This is what Mr. Fiedler means by "Gothic" and it is what he likes about *The Natural*. And so, while praising that book for its "lovely, absurd madness" he reproaches its author for the "denial of the marvellous" implicit in much of his later work, where, says Fiedler, "he turns back to the muted, drab world of the Depression as remembered two decades later." For Fiedler, "the denial of the marvellous" seems to be the gravest of apostasies, a dereliction of one's duty to be Gothic. But as I see it, the "marvellous" requires of its user the rarest of talents. The mode of it established by one writer seldom survives imitation by another (consider the fate of Kafka's imitators). And the presence in a novel of standardized Gothic machinery—for example the secret staircases and come-alive portraits in Hawthorne—often substitutes for true literary invention. In any case, so irrelevant are Gothic fancies to Malamud's sturdy characters, so little can they afford the luxury of a "lovely, absurd madness," that they are easily imagined as retorting: "So what's lovely about madness that we should play Ophelia?"

All this by way not so much of quizzing Mr. Fiedler, who has his better moments, but of trying to define Malamud, especially his differences from the "Gothic" or "wacky" strain in contemporary novels from *Catch 22* to *Naked Lunch* to *V*.

The differences are notable and tend to align Malamud with such a writer as J. F. Powers rather than with most of the Jewish-American novelists of today to whom he is generally compared. Like Powers, Malamud is a mildly conservative force in writing at present, a fact that he, like Powers, perhaps owes in part to his interest in the short story with its necessary economy and—in old-fashioned parlance—its highly "conscious art." Not for Powers or Malamud, in any case, those specialities of the modern Gothic or wacky novel: the "sick" hero, the "stateless" setting, the general effect of improvised narrative, the marathon sentence which, in its attempt to deliver instantaneously a total physical experience, leaves the reader feeling as if he had been frisked all over by a peculiarly assiduous cop. For the people of Malamud and Powers, Bellevue is out of bounds; they are not *that* sick. Moreover, a distinct localism rules their choice of settings; even when foreign, they are never "stateless" in the sense given to that word by Mary McCarthy in her account of *Naked Lunch.* In addition, neat patterns are traced on the reader's mind by the movement of the "story lines" of a Malamud or a Powers narrative; there is no effect of improvisation. And their prose avails itself of the special authority, so thoroughly exploited by the early Joyce, that is inherent in the short declarative sentence. Norman Podhoretz has noted Malamud's genius for getting the maximum authenticity from the maximum economy of such a statement as, "And there were days when he was sick to death of everything." Here are familiar words and a familiar rhythm for one who is "sick," presumably, in the sadly familiar way of hard-pressed people.

Malamud's ability to persuade us of the reality of his characters—their emotions, deeds, words, surroundings—remains astonishing. In most of the twelve stories that make up *Idiots First*, that ability is quite as evident as it was in *The Magic Barrel*, his earlier short story collection, and in those long stories (*The Assistant*, *A New Life*) we call his novels. There is no accounting for this elusive gift except by terms so trite as to seem like abstractions. His identification with his people tends to be perfect; and it is perfect because, on the one hand, they are mostly Jews of a certain class, as he is, and on the other (to quote Mr. Podhoretz further), they are "copied not from any models on earth but from an idea in the mind of Bernard Malamud." The idea brings about a grand simplification, or specialization, of historical fact. For one thing, Malamud's Jewish community is chiefly composed of people of East European origin. For another, they tend to retain, morally speaking, their immigrant status. Life is centered in the home and the workshop and remains tough and full of threats. The atmosphere is not that of the 1930's Depression alone, as Fiedler says, but that of the hard times ever immanent in the nature of things. His people may prosper for a while and within limits. But memories and connections continue to bind them to the Old World, in some cases to the world of the Old Testament where Jacob labors for Laban and Job suffers for everyone. Some of them, it is true, progress to the point of acquiring ineffably Anglo-Saxon first names ("Arthur Fidelman," for example). Some are found claiming that all-American privilege of the post-war period, "a year in Italy." But in Italy they become, or fear to become, immigrants all over again, and the old American theme of innocents abroad is updated. Golden Italy so confounds the professor of "The Maid's Shoes" that he dares open his heart to it not at all. The art student Arthur Fidelman is made of different stuff but not of stuff dependable enough to prevail against the glorious menace of golden Italy. In the story about him in *The Magic Barrel,* his first days in Rome were shown to be haunted by a crafty alter-ego (a "refugee from Israel") and Fidelman lost his notes on Giotto, the "Christian artist." In the two stories about him in *Idiots First* he is still being badly hustled in Italy and his few victories are painfully Pyrrhic.

The Fidelman stories are beautifully done and very funny. Something about them, however, suggests the rigors of a punitive expedition on the part of the author and possibly at his own expense. I remember his earlier tales of would-be artists and intellectuals—those dreary youths who lie all day on their rooming house beds trying to concentrate on the reading of *Madame Bovary* or on writing novels themselves. And I suspect that in these cases Malamud's identification with his world is carried beyond the point of perfection to a certain guilt and fear. His people seem to be watching him, rather than he them, to make sure that he doesn't get out of line. And then there is the story ("Black Is My Favorite Color") in which Mr. Malamud tries to motivate the love of a Jewish liquor dealer for a Negro woman by giving the liquor dealer a good deal of wry sensibility. "That was the night she wore a purple dress and I thought to myself, My God, what colors. Who paints that picture paints a masterpiece." This strikes me as a mere stereotype of Second Avenue folksiness. Nor are the author's powers of invention quite equal to the demands of the metaphysical fantasy which serves this volume as title story. Here an old man is pursued by Death until at last he acquires the courage to look Death squarely in the eye, thus winning the desired extension of his borrowed time. Meanwhile each has clarified his position to the other in the artificially racy speech of what sounds like a bull session. Challenged to explain his lack of "responsibility," Death says, "I ain't in the anthropo-morphic business." And the old man yells, "You bastard, don't you know what it means human?" Nor does it help that Malamud, humorizing, calls Death "Ginzburg." He sets out, perhaps, to disinfect Kafka's universe of its total tragedy and ends up approximating the whimsical affirmations of Paddy Chayefsky. Such are the occasional failures of a first rate tal-ent bent upon maintaining his "commitment" (in the slogan-eering phrase) to his own people and trying to be as positive as possible. In these cases, commitment, that very neces-sary stage in anyone's development towards freedom of self and imagination, seems to have become an end in itself, a commitment to commitment.

Among the many fine stories in *Idiots First,* two are very fine. One, "The German Refugee," simulates reportage rather than fable—perhaps it *is* reportage—and is the most pro-found rendering of the refugee theme I know. The other, "The Death of Me," is the epitome of the author's whole matter and manner—his fabling, as distinguished from his reporting, manner. Marcus, a former tailor, has risen to the level of clothier only to be harassed to death by the furious quarrels of his present tailor, a thin bitter hysterical Sicilian, and his presser, a beefy beery sobbing Pole. Their fury flows from their consciousness of old unhappy far-off things in their lives. And the prose in which Malamud renders their deliberate squalor and pain-wrung cries makes their troubles sound like all the troubles that ever were in the world.

To Malamud, Mr. Podhoretz says, "the Jew is humanity seen under the twin aspects of suffering and moral aspira-tion. Therefore any man who suffers greatly and also longs to be better than he is can be called a Jew." True, and the special appeal of "The Death of Me" comes from its giving the thumbscrew of this theme a decisive turn. Here are two men whose sufferings exceed those of Marcus the Jew until, realizing that they are beyond assimilation by his own ethos, he experiences the supreme suffering of total despair and gives up the ghost. There is true "madness" in this story—the madness not of Fiedler's prescription but of art.

1964

Difficulty
as Style

Although T. S. Eliot's early poems are now fairly intelligible to me, I still remember the trouble they gave me when I first saw them, in the twenties. Even then I felt in Eliot a remarkable pathos and distinction. But the poems as a whole were all the more bewildering because certain of their details and episodes seemed perfectly transparent. There were clear fragments of story, characters with lifelike names, recognizable references to history and literature. But these particulars existed in such strange combinations as to make me suspect even my moments of apparent illumination.

Then I began to study the critics who were explaining Eliot to the general reader, and I discovered that it was a mistake to read him for logical argument or continuous story. What appeared perversely arbitrary in his poems was in fact arbitrary on principle; they had the allusive structure of a dream. And thus in time I began to respond to the poems in such a way that it might be said I "understood" them. Yet this understanding helped me in only a general way to follow Eliot's later work or the work of other "difficult" poets. From poem to poem and poet to poet there was always for me a margin of obscurity which had to be overcome by study be-

This was originally a paper read at a session of The Modern Language Association.

fore I could say to myself that I "understood." Besides, the generation of Eliot was followed by the generation of Auden, and that in turn by the generation of Dylan Thomas; and although beliefs and methods altered considerably from one generation to the next, the factor of difficulty remained fairly constant.

Now much of the writing about modern poetry has of course been polemical and has centered around just this question of its obscurity. As a result, its obscurity has come to be regarded as an accidental feature which could be overcome if the poet were more cooperative or the reader less lazy. A critic like Max Eastman blames the willful snobbishness of poets who could be more lucid if they wished. A critic like Allen Tate replies that the poetry only *appears* difficult, and does so because we have "lost the art of reading" or because we try to read all poetry in the light of habits and expectations formed by a taste for Keats and Shelley. Mr. Tate even maintains that "the complainant does not understand Donne or Marvell any better than he understands Eliot." But it is hard to say whether this latter statement is true or not: so much hinges on the word "understand," to which critics like Mr. Tate, influenced by the intricate nature of modern poetry itself, have given a new and complex meaning. And they have so impressed us with this meaning that even a writer like Sidney Hook, who is not a literary critic, can say (and quite rightly), "The effort to discover what the poet is trying to say contributes to the process of understanding the created whole."

But there is another possible approach to the question of poetic difficulty. Instead of trying to explain it by the failings of individual poets or of individual readers, we may conceive of it as a regular feature of the modern poetic *style*. Many imponderables enter into the formation of any such style, but surely a style is in part determined by the kind of relations that exist between the art and the culture at large, between the artists and the society. From this point of view the lazy reader and the aloof poet must both be taken into account because both are elements in the cultural situation out of which the difficult style of poetry springs.

I am all the more inclined to regard obscurity as a special trait of modern verse because to my knowledge it has never been much of a problem to past critics. They have complained of it but seldom, and then as merely an occasional and superficial blemish. Horace said in the *Ars Poetica*, "Brevis esse labore: obscurus fio"—"I labor to be brief and grow obscure"—implying that obscurity is simply a deplorable by-product of the compressive process of metrical composition. Even the somewhat difficult John Donne seems to have shared, at least in theory, this purely rhetorical view of the problem. He remarks in one of his sermons: "It is true, thou mayst find some dark places in the Scriptures; and *Est silentii species obscuritas*. To speake darkly and obscurely is a kinde of silence, I were as good not be spoken to, as not be made to understand that which is spoken."

Thus for Donne obscurity is "a kinde of silence," or as we would say today, "a failure of communication." In nineteenth-century criticism of Shakespeare, however, critics begin to see in the tangled passages of the later plays a witty and allusive virtue. But it remained for T. S. Eliot, in his influential early essay "The Metaphysical Poets," to characterize obscurity as a positive, one might almost say, a principled, element of modern verse. "We can only say that it appears likely that poets in our civilization, as it exists at present, must be *difficult*. Our civilization comprehends great variety and complexity, and this variety and complexity, playing upon a refined sensibility, must produce various and complex results. The poet must become more and more comprehensive, more allusive, more indirect, in order to force, to dislocate if necessary, language into its meaning."

Since Mr. Eliot's essay is not intended as a formal defense of poetic difficulty, his remark ought not to be taken as a formal argument. Even as a partial explanation, however, it appears to me of limited value. If cultural complexity in a merely quantitative sense were all that was in question here, then it would be possible to argue—indeed it has often been argued—that other ages had witnessed a comparable complexity without exhibiting any such drastic complication of poetic style as we have at present.

Or did Mr. Eliot mean his remark on the complexity of our civilization as more than a description of this civilization—as in fact a *judgment* on it? Strictures on this civilization are extremely common and extremely vehement in Eliot, and also in the work of other poets of the difficult school as far back as Rimbaud, who was one of its founders. May not the difficult style, then, be regarded as a kind of implied *judgment* on modern life, the complexity of which is only one of the terrors it holds for artists? May not this style, with its ambiguity, its allusiveness, its structure of myths derived sometimes from private experience or from relatively new and inaccessible sciences, be another symptom of that "alienated" consciousness which manifests itself in so many ways in modern literature?

I wonder, in short, if a high degree of difficulty is not an aspect of the modern poetic style just as a peculiarly brilliant and aggressive clarity was a stylistic aspect of the school of Pope. We know that by and large the school of Pope was sympathetic towards the society of its age and regarded itself as the champion of accepted values against dunces and outlaws; whereas contemporary poets are the heirs of a century-old tension between artists and society. Of course I do not mean that modern poets *deliberately* obscure their meaning in order to be rude to a world they cannot abide. It is not a question of individual poets and their motives, but of a general style, of which no single poet was the inventor and in which those who participate do so without necessarily having full awareness of its broader cultural implications. Indeed, so prevalent is the style today that poets with only a lesser grievance against the modern world—poets like E. E. Cummings and Wallace Stevens—are no less difficult than Eliot or Rimbaud. And finally, the difficult style is not confined to poetry but is present in painting, in certain works of prose fiction, and in other contemporary arts.

What I have been saying is not intended as a "theory" of difficulty in poetry; and considered as a contribution to the polemics over this issue it certainly begs the question. The opponents of modern poetry will say that if difficulty is inherent in the style, then it is the style that must be assailed or defended. This I happen to think is true. Not the obscurity of the poetry but the poetry itself ought to be the issue, if we assume that by study and experience modern poems can, with whatever tax on our patience, be made to yield up reasonably satisfactory meanings. In short there is no very sensible *a priori* defense of this factor of difficulty; it is defensible only in so far as it is an element in a poetry which can on other counts be shown to be great poetry. For poetry has often had to make its way against common sense: the early reviews of Keats are very persuasive so long as we don't read Keats. Similarly, the obscurity of modern poetry may often seem to be unreasonable, antisocial, even insane; but out of that poetry have come Rimbaud's *Illuminations,* Eliot's *The Waste Land,* Yeats's Byzantine poems, Stevens's *Harmonium*—works which are not, surely, unreasonable or antisocial or insane but are great examples of poetic literature.

1945

The
Muse
as House
Guest

Young America can still be heard singing, by anyone with
very sensitive auditory equipment. Writing verse, publishing
volumes, giving public readings from their work, winning
prizes and fellowships, a lot of young men and women continue to go about the business of being poets. If this is news
to most readers, lost as I imagine most readers are in contemplation of "the novel," it is partly because the poems of the
young make little clamor. Resourceful leaders are lacking to
them, and self-advocacy in the form of critical pronounce-
ments is generally not a part of their business.

Yet the younger poets are not without ample public support, as I gather from the biographical data included in the
several recent volumes I have at hand. Honors abound: if a
poet is unlucky enough to miss out on one of the Borestone
Mountain Awards he may still capture the Glascock Memorial Prize or the less lugubrious-sounding Lamont Poetry Selection, bestowed annually by the Academy of American
Poets. Besides this group, a great many lesser societies for
the encouragement of verse writing flourish, whether in
Atlanta, Worcester, Denver, or New York City. Even the
employees of the federal government have one, named The
Federal Poets. In some respects, moreover, conditions of publication have become increasingly favorable to the little-

known poet. It is true that the more prominent publishers continue to list just about the same judiciously small number of poetry "titles" that they have always listed. But some of the university presses (Michigan, Indiana) now include volumes of verse among their scholarly items. Then the flourishing paperback gets many poets into public circulation, often in an attractive as well as inexpensive format (e.g. the delightful volume Evergreen Books has made out of James Broughton's *True & False Unicorn*).

As for magazines that print respectable poetry, there is always, for the *poème bien fait*—and not too radically original —pre-eminently *The New Yorker*. The small audience magazines that give much space to verse are now more numerous than anyone except the harassed librarian in the periodical room could imagine. *Broom, Blast, Blues* and the other ancestral little magazines have, as it were, multiplied like minks through the subsequent decades. Unfamiliar names crowd the acknowledgment pages of many volumes. For the right to reprint her work, one poet renders thanks to *Spirit, Voices, Quicksilver, The Step Ladder, Kaleidograph, Poetry Digest, The Lyric, Variegation, American Weave, University of Kansas Review, Prairie Schooner, Yankee, The Bronxville Villager, Educational Forum, American Bard,* and *The Fawnlight*.

The younger poets are not only richly honored and thoroughly published, they are distinctly a job-holding generation. A census-taker would have no trouble with them when it came to specifying their occupations. Among the contributors to *New Poems By American Poets 2,* a representative paperback anthology edited by Rolfe Humphries, only oldtimers like E. E. Cummings and Vincent McHugh are listed as unemployed. Nor are the remainder of Humphries' contributors to be found exclusively where one might expect to find them: in university posts. A young poet today may be in anything from occupational therapy to the Catholic priest-hood to the U. S. Forest Service. But the classroom certainly claims the majority of them—so many that Robert Frost is at pains to defend them in a foreword to *New Poets of England and America,* declaring that "poetry has been a great concern of schools all down the ages." Such, however, is the eagerness of editors for fresh material that they seek it from poets who are still in the undergraduate stage. One young man whose work occupies a third of a volume with two co-versifiers is advertised as "studying with Robert Lowell at Boston University" while a second is "studying Classics with Dr. Roger Hornsby" (university unnamed).

So far as my data go, the record for continuous recognition and uninterrupted occupation is held by a twenty-seven year old poet whose first volume has recently been given to the world by a university press. The jacket reads in part: "After graduating in 1952 from Amherst College, where he won the Colin Armstrong Poetry Prize, he was employed as a research analyst with the National Security Agency in Washington, D. C. In 1953 he was drafted into the army and served in the Counter Intelligence Corps until his discharge in May, 1955. While in the army, he applied for a Fulbright scholarship to study in England and was awarded one to Worcester College, Oxford." No grass grew under these winged feet, even "while in the army."

No doubt the favorable—if that is the word for it— economic situation of recent years has affected the tone and substance of the poetry written by the young generation. So has the domesticity which is now made easily possible, if it is not actually encouraged, by their job holding status. A verse writing father and husband is less likely than a muse ridden bachelor to arrive in the classroom with a hangover and his papers uncorrected. But marriage is obviously an attractive as well as advisable state for the young poets, and it provides them with a large stock of poetic subjects. House, wife, children, parents, pets, gardens, summer resorts, travel *en famille* make up the unromantic romance of this poetry and equip the poet with a special kind of consciousness—what it is I shall try later on to make clear. For this observation there is not only the internal evidence of the poems but—again— the evidence supplied by compilers of biographical notes. The compilers seem to be in love with family happiness these days and like to name the poet's wife, enumerate his children, and offer other homely details. We learn of one poet that "while there [in Cambridge, England], he was married, in 1954, to —— who traveled all the way from Missouri for the purpose." Missouri *is* a far piece to travel from, for any purpose; and it is interesting to discover that another poet bears a different name "in private life" and that "three children and many more dogs share her interest, but she admits she 'can't communicate with cats.' "

New Poets of England and America assists us in penetrating the apparent anonymity, not to say nonentity, of the youthful band of men and women who make verse under these circumstances. The volume has been carefully edited, probably with some such purpose as this in mind, by three of the young poets themselves: Donald Hall, Robert Pack, and Louis Simpson. The editors include work by poets ranging in age from about twenty-two to about forty. The presence of some of Robert Lowell's truly impassioned poetry allows us to see how little impassioned—in any usual sense—the work of the younger writers is, and so encourages us to look in it for other qualities. Representatives of the West Coast School (the "Beats") are not, so far as I can make out, included; and while this omission makes for unity in the volume, it also makes for a certain monotony, as well as for an incomplete roster of "the new poets." Nor is Frost's foreword, good as it is in itself, a substitute for the introduction which the editors might better have written for themselves, thereby setting forth, as Frost does not dream of doing, their intentions and claims. Does an anthology of verse have to be sponsored like a television program? If so, Frost's is the best of brand names; and it is noteworthy that the young now acknowledge, as the young did not always do, his mastery. But the relation in this case, as in that of the young generation with other established poets and artists, does not seem to me to be a very active or helpful relation. It is the soothing one of homage eagerly given and complacently received; the atmosphere is that of a congenial party rather than of a working studio. (Indeed, the poem of homage to this or that authority is among the stock subjects.) And for all Frost says of "schools," it was not as a poet in residence or a Brooks and Warren instructor that he learned to write "An Old Man's Winter Night" or "A Servant to Servants."

A bursting rocket photographed against a black sky is on the cover of *New Poets*. Shall we say that the fireworks are all on the cover? It depends on what is meant by fireworks. In the contents of the volume there is little pyrotechnic display in the form of verbal or typographic experiments. The presiding muse here is unassertive, intelligent, amusing, voluble, company-conscious—the perfect guest. The scene tends to be indoors, the mode of communication is conversation, the talk is generally good. If this state of poetic manners excludes shows of unique energy and vision, it does so deliberately rather than furtively. And one of the contributors, Adrienne Rich, seems to allude to the whole situation when she ends "The Celebration in the Plaza" with

> The viceroy of fireworks goes his way,
> Leaving us with a sky so dull and bare
> The crowd thins out: what conjures them to stay?
>
> The road is cold with dew, and by and by
> We see the constellations overhead.
> *But is that all?* some little children cry.
> *All we have left,* their pedagogues reply.

The viceroy of fireworks goes his way; the emperor of ice cream is dead. All we have left is a rueful recollection of their exploits. So say the pedagogues. But their dogmatic gloom is belied by the appeal of the poem itself, which says more than it asserts.

The characteristics of this poem are, generally speaking, the characteristics of all Miss Rich's work and of the best work of her generation. The language is neither systematically colloquial, as Frost's language once tended to be, nor alternately colloquial and conceptual, as Eliot's was in his early poems; nor does it burst into a dazzling spray of fantastication as Stevens's was apt to do. Miss Rich seems to have access to some common style, a language which she and her contemporaries all tend to speak easily, with a minimum of individual inflection. It permits them to retain the "conversational tone," that all but universal idiom of modernist poetry, and yet to sound it without the apparent exercise of any strict selective principle. So too with the structure of the verse, which generally scans but is free enough to allow the musical phrase, as distinguished from the metrical foot, a certain autonomy. But the way of this common style with metaphor is probably its most definitive trait. The proud, self-sufficient "image" or "symbol" of modernist poetry, subduing all local or random figuration to its central purpose, and offering to the reader the allurement of a dark glass turned on an enigmatic universe, is largely gone from this poetry. With it is gone the modernist assertion of the supremacy of imagination and the artist. To claim access to an *anima mundi* or to the omniscience of a Tiresias, in the manner of a Yeats or an Eliot, would occur to none of these poets, if I know them. Indeed, figures of speech are now apt to be announced by a candid "like" or "as"; the homely simile is back; experience is fancified rather than transformed; readers are cordially invited to share in the processes.

The muse as desirable visitor is eminently and happily Miss Rich's muse. A woman in a non-feminist age, an artist in a time that is not *conspicuously* creative, she makes poetry out of a sense of limitations, is equable without the accusing calm of the self-accepting, wise without being a young owl. Her "Living In Sin" describes a studio love affair from the viewpoint of a mildly domestic-minded girl. It is in twenty-seven lines of limpid unrhymed verse and is an admirable work of this poet and this time.

Some of the men poets are more ambitious than Miss Rich but they are not often better. On many of them, too, acute feelings of limitation are patently at work; and the domestic status, in those who have it, is apt to induce the peculiar form of restrictive consciousness on which I remarked above. The poems that express it, in their several ways, are among the most original in the various volumes. This consciousness helps to do duty for the highly developed sense of role which good poets generally have and which does not seem to come easily to these younger poets. By sense of role I mean the kind of postures assumed by Whitman when he is being the cosmic reporter to whom all things are copy, or by Emily Dickinson when she beautifully queens it in her suffering universe, or by Ezra Pound when he is the Promethean exhorter, or by Frost and Stevens when they take up opposite but complementary positions toward the world's work, becoming respectively the visionary farmer and the Sunday poet with a Monday morning conscience. This dramatic conception of self vis-à-vis the reader and the world is, I suggest, largely alien to the younger poets, and the absence of it is probably more damaging to their work than the mere blackout of modernist fireworks. It is here, possibly, that the security provided by their common style and material well-being plays them false. They appear content to be just poets together, indifferent to the histrionic claims that poetry makes on a culture when poetry is a major art.

In that restrictive consciousness of theirs, however, there is, in certain cases, something like an emergent sense of role. It is apt to express itself in a confessional form which has its antecedents in Yeats, Eliot and Auden. But the confessor is now increasingly finite and personal. Saying I, he usually means his literal self in all its literal daily reality. "Mirror, mirror on the wall, / Who is Donald Andrew Hall?" inquires Donald Hall; and in another poem (both of them in *New Poems*) he locates himself still more exactly: "I sit upon a changing porch and think / ideas about the insubstantial wood, / that I may make real porches out of ink." Hall has other subjects and some expert verse; but a certain blunt assertion of self, as of a real poet in a real garden, place and hour and weather specified, state of mind clarified and moral drawn, does tend to characterize his performance. He has a more free-spirited counterpart in W. D. Snodgrass, who also makes poetry out of a very tangible personal relation to children, job, landscape and even to his surname ("Snodgrass is walking through the universe"). Pressure of circumstance makes this poet's consciousness half assertive, half uneasy. Out of the compound comes, now and then, something freshly comic, for this American poet has affinities with the comparable English school of Kingsley Amis, in his poems and novels, and Philip Larkin, in his poems. Divested, like them, of the myths, masks and ideologies of modernism, Mr. Snodgrass inhabits a kind of spiritual nudist colony where, embarrassed in spite of himself, he braves it out with grins, quips and little shivers of pathos. But he is never as indignant, or as funny, as Amis is capable of being; nor does he possess the crepitating moral sensibility that invests Larkin's verse with its faint appealing music. Snodgrass's rhymes and rhythms are unfaltering, and his command of rather bouncy colloquialisms is invincible. *New Poets* contains several selections from *Heart's Needle*, Snodgrass's long poem about a child lost to the poet-father by reason of a divorce. Expressions of grief and guilt here sound with a spare eloquence in stanzas of considerable intricacy and, often, beauty. Everything goes well until the poet, remembering that he is an oddball and funny man, refers to himself as an "absentee bread-winner" or recalls how he and his child once roasted hot dogs on "old coat-hangers." Snodgrass, too, is a university teacher, and in another selection, "April Inventory," he writes: "The sleek expensive girls I teach,/ Younger and pinker every year,/ Bloom gradually out of reach." (Fortunately, one thinks, for the propriety of the classroom.) Again: "I taught myself to name my name,/ To bark back, loosen love with crying,/ To ease my woman so she came."

A pose similar to Snodgrass', though without his unfortunate swagger, is occasionally struck by Howard Nemerov and Reed Whittemore, both represented in *New Poets*. In "The Vacuum" Nemerov writes: "The house is so quiet now/ The vacuum cleaner sulks in the corner closet,/ Its bag limp as a stopped lung, its mouth/ Grinning into the floor, maybe at my/ Slovenly life, my dog-dead youth." In "A Week of Doodles" Whittemore is no less humorously despondent over the failure in him of the poetic afflatus. He is "waiting and waiting and waiting/ For something to say." Meanwhile, what he does produce is "Neither major nor minor but merely (an old kind) doodle." But doodle, he goes on to say, has its uses. "Doodle is waiting raised to a fine art." Maybe.

The role of the academic schlemiel is a slight one at best, and the present tyranny of "light verse" contributes to its further attenuation. It has the painful effect of stifling any emotion beyond what can be experienced while one is being watched by a wife or a child or a class of students or—as it sometimes appears—by the poem one is writing. It produces a nervous intensity of observation, a poverty of vision, and seems to render impossible any connection between poetry and the realm of general ideas.

An historical as opposed to a personal account of the role is given by Louis Simpson, a poet of greater scope than most and of formidable technical skill. I am quoting "The Silent Generation" in *New Poems*. It was his contemporaries, Simpson says, who "put the Devil down" (meaning Hitler) with great enthusiasm—

> But now our occupation
> Is gone, our education
> Is wasted on the town.
> We lack enthusiasm.

Life seems a mystery;
It's like the play a lady
Told me about: "It's not . . .
It doesn't have a plot,"
She said, "It's history."

It probably is just history—the Cold War and all it implies
—that has caused and is causing the impoverishment of the
creative spirit, and not only in poetry and in Mr. Simpson's
generation. Still, single poems may be superior to the general
state of poetry, and individual talents may hold promise of
development. In the volumes at hand there are superior
poems by several writers, including William Jay Smith,
Richard Wilbur, William Meredith, Philip Booth, John Hollander, and Anthony Hecht. In Hollander and Hecht, the
pleasure in wit and musical structure replaces any acute preoccupation with self and history. And then there is W. S.
Merwin, a poet who seems to have arrived on the contemporary scene out of another world. It is not yet a clearly defined
location, and the atmosphere of it can be windy as well as
airy. But Love is there a passion instead of a slogan, and
verse shows an elemental confidence in itself, transcending
jobs, awards, fellowships, history and the other conditions of
its making.

1958

Note

Since the above remarks were written, the poetry scene has
definitely brightened. Robert Lowell has reached a consider-

able public with his *Life Studies* and *For the Union Dead.* John Berryman's *77 Dream Songs,* and the volumes of verse published just before and just after his death by Theodore Roethke, have further liberated the muse. In John Ashbery, Kenneth Koch and others of the so-called "New York School" we have, moreover, a new avant-garde.

1965

The
Battle
of Lowell

When Robert Lowell's first book of poems appeared, about fifteen years ago, it seemed to me and most others that he was the heir of all the poetic ages, at least from Milton to Hart Crane. He could write with the abandon of Crane and yet make immediate sense like Milton. He proved to have a real subject and a real place in the world at just about the moment when Auden, for one, seemed in danger of forfeiting his place and subject and becoming a globe-trotting commentator. Mr. Lowell's subject was of the largest; it had to do with history and the self. And although this was also the subject of some of his great elder fellow-poets, he had special reasons for laying claim to it too. Boston, city of historic battles and embattled selves, was his birthright as well as his birthplace; his family history was in some degree its history. And so the Boston of the old families, with its monuments, its Public Garden, its favorite suburbs and resorts, its own Atlantic Ocean, became the main setting of his poems—his Lake Country, his Yoknapatawpha.

In his early lyrics and monologues Lowell went to work on this faded locale as Faulkner had done on his faded South. He took the city's latter-day unreality to himself, determined to restore to both of them an awareness of their common past, their common position in the universe, their common fall from grace. In his own mind he revived the vehemence of the old wars and controversies which had made Boston Boston. A Lowell and not a Lowell, an escaped Bostonian, a puritan turned Catholic, a Catholic whose puritanism made him continue to worry his new faith, he rejoiced in his contradictions, including the pain of them. The hurtful exhilaration of the experience was written all over the style of his poetry. The muscular verbs, packed epithets, rushing enjambments, fierce play of wit, persistent interplay of heroic and mockheroic modes made for a bravura medium awesome in its magnificence and a little relentless in its intensity. In this verse Boston was certainly brought alive, but as Boston might be on a Judgment Day presided over by some half-pitying, half-jeering divinity. An atmosphere of extremity and futility prevailed. Jesus walked the waters on Easter Day to ferry Grandfather Winslow to Acheron in a swan boat from the Public Garden. A Concord farmer trying to kiss his wife saw himself growing scales like Eden's serpent. The Atlantic was fouled with dead sailors and itched to possess nuns and other virgins. A man dreamed, only dreamed, of writing the *Aeneid*.

In the apocalyptic climate of the 1940's Robert Lowell became the leading poet of his generation. He wrote as if poetry were still a major art and not merely a venerable pastime which ought to be perpetuated. But there were difficulties in his extreme position and style. Randall Jarrell, an intensely sympathetic critic, once summed them up by speaking of the contagion of violence, the excess of willful effort, in Lowell's work. "As a poet Mr. Lowell sometimes doesn't trust enough in God and tries to do everything for himself." It may be that he didn't trust enough in nature and human life. His native place and chosen setting offered little that appealed to his senses and affections as intimately as, say, the southern

Negroes and poor whites, with their work-worn hands, sun-seasoned shacks and other attributes, appealed to Faulkner. Nor did religion seem to be a substitute for the tempering effects of such immediacies, except as religion was embodied in character—the character, for example, of the proud Mother Superior in his fine monologue, "Mother Marie Therese." Here as in many other poems, like "The Drunken Fisherman" and "Falling Asleep Over the Aeneid," Lowell's corrosively tragic imagination found its form. Elsewhere it tended to run riot very much as Faulkner's rather similar imagination has occasionally done.

A consciousness of these old difficulties seems to be implied in *Life Studies*, a volume made up of new poems together with a few older ones and an autobiographical fragment in prose. The new style is conspicuously barer than the old style, and the poet is more intent now on understanding the causes of his tragic imagination than on flaunting it. He seems no longer to seek support from theology. The opening poem, "Beyond the Alps," about a train journey from Rome to Paris, appears to record his apostasy; and there is further evidence in the absence of religious feeling and imagery from the poems themselves. A frankly de-converted poet is a rarity in these times; but the poetry here is not about the drama—if any—of de-conversion. It is about the aftermath. After such knowledge, what forgiveness? Guilt, remorse, feelings of loss? Not at all. With scarcely a backward glance at all that, Lowell addresses himself to his life studies like a painter or sculptor who wants to ground his art more firmly in the observation of things as they are in the natural world. But the title of the volume has, of course, only limited application. Nature for Lowell is his habitat, heritage and present existence; and his scrutiny of these things is anything but objective. More than his former religious commitments, these things vex his memory and confine his ego. Two poems describe actual incarcerations: in a mental hospital where the poet was a patient, and in a jail where he served a term as a conscientious objector during the last war.

It is still a dark day in Boston even though it is no longer Judgment Day. Hardly anything is what it should be even though the discrepancies now produce more humor and quizzical tenderness than fierce wit. The book abounds in second-class Lowells, in mothers who were unequal to their pretensions when alive and to their black and gold coffins when dead; in fathers who, though naval officers, preferred automobiles to ships and whose "Sunday mornings were given to useful acts such as lettering three new galvanized garbage cans: R.T.S. LOWELL—U.S.N."; and in only sons who had chronic asthma, chronic truculence and got themselves expelled from the Public Garden. Lowell's merciless anatomy of his parents is matched by his merciless account of himself. The volume that begins with "Beyond the Alps" ends with "Skunk Hour," a poem in which he claims affinity with the little scavengers of the title. Does the poet give the impression of being unjust to himself, as well as unfair to skunks?

His persistent refusal of happiness, his constant indulgence of a guilty conscience, would make a monotonous spectacle if it were not for a knowing humor and a distinct poise of style in the self-proclaimed offender. For Lowell is not only the hunger artist practicing an art of famine because he doesn't like food; he *knows* he is something like that and he makes a conscious role of it. The prose memoirs are the most triumphant example of his essential composure. The surface of them is all anecdote and caricature, malign and dazzling;

but the interior is solid analysis of a family, a society, a period; and when completed the work should excel any poet's autobiography since Yeats's. The portraits and memories in verse are exciting in their search for a cadenced as opposed to a strictly metrical medium. Like *Mauberley*, Pound's sequence of satiric scenes and portraits, including self-portraits, from London life, they add up to a marvellous comedy of secular damnation—in, for the most part, Boston.

1959

Kenneth
Koch's
Poetry

Thank You and Other Poems is a selection from Kenneth Koch's shorter poems. The volume includes none of his plays nor any passages from *Ko* or his other more or less lengthy narratives. The omission is perhaps a pity. Mr. Koch's plays have a special appeal: they give a peculiarly succinct expression to his enormously animated conception of things. Yet his better poems convey that conception too, in their own way.

Koch's position in modern poetry is not easy to determine. It may help to begin by pairing him with a long-established older poet to whom his relations are obviously close enough in some respects, and absurdly distant enough in others, to be instructive. In part he is one of those "literalists of the imagination" who are commended by Marianne Moore in a well-known poem and whose principles are exemplified in her own work. Like Miss Moore, Koch is fond of making poetry out of poetry-resistant stuff. Locks, lipsticks, business letterheads, walnuts, lunch and fudge attract him; so do examples of inept slang, silly sentiment, brutal behavior and stereotyped exotica and erotica. Whatever helps him to "exalt the imagination at the expense of its conventional appearances" (Richard Blackmur's formula for Marianne Moore) is welcome, although not to the exclusion of such familiar poetic properties as the sun, the sea, trees and girls.

But Koch never submits either kind of phenomenon to any Moore-like process of minute and patient scrutiny. He is eminently an activist, eagerly participating in, rather than merely observing, the realm of locks and fudge. And if, like Marianne Moore, he is always springing surprises, he does not spring them as if he were handing you a cup of tea. Her finely conscious demureness is not for him. For him, the element of surprise, and the excitement created by it, are primary and absolute. In short, "life" does not present itself to Kenneth Koch as a picture or symbol or collector's item. "Life" talks, sighs, grunts and sometimes sings; it is a drama, largely comic, in which there are parts for everyone and everything, and all the parts are speaking parts.

> Filmed in the morning I am
> A pond. Dreamed of at night I am a silver
> Pond. Who's wading through me? Ugh!

Those pigs! But they have their say elsewhere in the poem called "Farm's Thoughts."

The thirty-one poems in this volume were written during the past ten or twelve years and are very uneven in quality. Some of this unevenness may be the result of a defective sense of proportion, even a defective ear, on the poet's part. Mostly, it seems to spring from a certain abandon inherent in his whole enterprise. Apparently Koch is determined to put the reality back into Joyce's "reality of experience," to restore the newness to Pound's "Make it New," while holding ideas of poetry and of poetic composition that are essentially different from those of the classic modern writers. In his attempt to supersede—or transform—those writers, Koch has drawn upon far-flung sources. They range from Kafka to certain recent French poets (including Surrealists), to Whitman,

Gertrude Stein, William Carlos Williams and others in the native book.

Koch's general aims are made clear—well, *pretty* clear—in a dialogue poem called "On the Great Atlantic Rainway" which starts the present volume off. A T. S. Eliot character is uncomfortably present at the exchange of views: "an old man in shorts, blind, who has lost his way in the filling station." A wise old Yeatsian bird, also on hand, finds occasion to remark: "And that is our modern idea of fittingness." But our poet raises these ghosts only to shoo them away. His own idea of fittingness is to shed all formulas, "to go from the sun/ Into love's sweet disrepair," to await whatever forms of "unsyntactical beauty might leap up" beneath the world's rainways. In other words, he will flee the sunlight of approved poetic practice, staking his poetic chances on whatever wonders may turn up in the wet weather ("rainways") of *unapproved* poetic practice. He will talk to himself, improvise, consult his dreams, cherish the *trouvaille,* and misprize the well-wrought poem.

Such, as I make it out, is Kenneth Koch's unprogrammatic program (or a part of it), and the calamitous possibilities in it are obvious. Like the similar program of certain of the Beats, it could turn the writing of poetry into a form of hygiene. It could and does: some of Koch's efforts, like many of theirs, suggest the breathing exercises of a particularly deep-breasted individual. "Fresh Air," his most overt attack on the poetic Establishment, is half a witty skirmish, half an interminable harangue. The Unconscious, moreover, is not the dependable innovator it is often alleged to be. It really dotes on clichés; and those unsyntactical beauties supposedly lurking beneath Koch's rainway sometimes turn out to be discarded umbrellas. Consulting the sybil of the unconscious, he occasionally gets stuck with large mouthfuls of predigested images and with lines of verse that make no known kind of music. "I want spring. I want to turn like a mobile/ In a new fresh air." Spring? Mobiles? Fresh air? He might start by freshening up his allusions. "I love you as a sheriff searches for a walnut/ That will solve a murder case unsolved for years. . . ." Back to the Varsity Show with him. And if his verse is sometimes lacking in the delights of a reliable style, it also offers few of the conveniences of a consistent lucidity. To me his idiom is often a Linear B that remains to be cracked.

But having deciphered quite a lot of it, I feel hopeful that the rest will come clear in time. And for the silly sheriff and the boring mobile there are compensations. There is "a wind that blows from/ The big blue sea, so shiny so deep and so unlike us." Marvelous. And there is the strange excitement aroused by this beginning of a poem called "Summery Weather."

> One earring's smile
> Near the drawer
> And at night we gambling
> At that night the yacht on Venice
> Glorious too, oh my heavens
> See how her blouse was starched up

"Summery Weather" is a poem of only twenty-five lines in which is concentrated much of the romance of travel as well as much of the banality of that romance. No wonder the earring smiles.

There are several poems of greater length in the volume, two of the best of them being "The Artist" and "The Railway Stationery." Both can be read as portraits of the artist, possibly as fanciful self-portraits of Koch himself in two of his guises. The first is about a sort of mad Action Painter or Constructivist Sculptor who uses the American landscape as his canvas or showroom. A man of inexhaustible creative powers and many commissions, he consults only his sybil, coming up with a series of colossi which are, it appears, neither artifacts nor art objects. And all the time he records in his journals various Gide-like reflections on the ecstasies and pangs of the creative life. "May 16th. With what an intense joy I watched the installation of the *Magician of Cincinnati* today, in the Ohio River, where it belongs, and which is so much a part of my original scheme." The *Magician of Cincinnati,* a contraption of heroic size, happens to render navigation on the Ohio impossible. But never mind. The Artist will soon attempt something quite different. A good modernist, he never repeats himself—thank God.

"The Railway Stationery" is about a sheet of company letterhead. Engraved on it is a half-inch locomotive which, when the paper is looked at from the reverse side, seems to be backing up; and there is a railway clerk who writes on the stationery, very carefully, a letter beginning "Dear Mary." This poem, composed in blank verse as transparent as the stationery, as touchingly flat as the salutation, may be Kenneth Koch's offering to the artist (lower case) in everyone and everything.

1963

Leavis
and
Lawrence

F. R. Leavis is an influential English scholar and critic, and how provocative he can be on the subject of prose fiction we already know from *The Great Tradition,* his widely read study of the English novel. The present volume has the advantage of forming a sort of sequel to that one, and in Lawrence considered as a novelist Mr. Leavis has a little-explored subject—one, moreover, which he knows thoroughly and for which he has enormous enthusiasm. Yet his enthusiasm does not prove to be contagious, for *D. H. Lawrence: Novelist,* with all its promise and its undoubted virtues, is in many ways a tedious and unconvincing performance. The reasons for this are fairly obvious, and before considering them we had better make a brief accounting of the virtues.

These consist in Leavis' comprehensive feeling for Lawrence's greatness and his willingness to demonstrate it by a minute examination of Lawrence's performance in the novel, the genre on which that writer set most store. It is Leavis' opinion that Lawrence excelled at the long narrative but this is not the more general opinion. T. S. Eliot, as Leavis never tires of reminding us, has admitted Lawrence's genius but refused to credit him with the very qualities which would make that genius effective in the larger forms of literature. He has denied him intelligence, culture, humor and

art; and a similarly invidious view has prevailed widely in
criticism. The view may not be so entrenched as Leavis
thinks, nor owe what currency it has to the sort of Eliotish
conspiracy he conjures up. Yet the denigration of Lawrence
has been common enough to justify the defense of him, and
it is just on those disputed points that Leavis' defense is centered.

Where Lawrence has been charged with cultural barbarism, Leavis claims for him "a marvelous intelligence" and
"an astringent delicacy" of feeling for human relationships;
and these qualities, he maintains, were fostered by the
strictly English traditions in which Lawrence was reared. As
opposed to the assertion that he was only intermittently an
artist, Leavis acclaims his "marvelous rendering of the movement of life"; and if he never quite says what this rendering
of life may be as distinguished from what he calls "the mere
pondering of experience" (pondering seems not to be a part
of life for him), he does insist with much cogency that Lawrence's power of art rested on conscious principles which
were effectively present in all his major fiction, long as well
as short.

This may be described—fairly, it is hoped—as the minimum intention of *D. H. Lawrence: Novelist;* and allowing
for Leavis' exaggerations, the intention was altogether worth
carrying out. To be sure, his estimate of *The Rainbow* and
Women in Love, the two most ambitious novels, may seem
unduly high. Yet he makes clear Lawrence's purposes in
them, points out their indubitably fine moments, and is generally more interesting on the subject than those who merely
repeat: "Lawrence was not a novelist." And the same probably holds for his inordinate, as it seems to me, evaluation of
that writer in relation to his contemporaries. Not content to

reclaim him from partial neglect, Leavis contends that Lawrence is "incomparably the greatest writer in English of our time," excelling everyone else as a novelist, a master of the short story, and even as a critic. Yet if a writer is as remarkable as Lawrence certainly was, this exaltation of him is not in itself harmful. No doubt it is better than the not infrequent practice of malice or condescension toward him.

In exalting Lawrence, however, Leavis also debases other writers of Lawrence's and our time, notably Eliot and James Joyce. He persecutes those whom he conceives to have been the persecutors of Lawrence, and it is this violence which makes his pages acrid with the smoke of old feuds and goes far toward spoiling his whole enterprise. So extravagant are his claims and charges that what appears to have been planned as a grand offensive—like Shaw's in favor of Ibsen, or Ruskin's for Gothic architecture—turns into a protracted and wearisome campaign of defense. Between struggling to put his subject in the best light, and contending with his own enemies, Leavis gets between Lawrence and ourselves and is seldom at ease with either.

These are "tactical" exertions, as he calls them, and they are one thing. More serious is the way that, in his own irascible consciousness of isolation, he isolates Lawrence from the genius of modernity which helped to ignite his flame just as it did that of Eliot and Joyce, a "tradition" in itself, what was, after all, thus constituting the tradition of modernity. For Leavis, the tracing of traditions is a means not of clarifying literary relationships and indicating preferences but of drawing the line in blood between creative minds. He insists that if you admire Lawrence, who was all life-enhancing "art", you cannot admire Joyce, who was all life-denying "contrivances." What arrogant nonsense, one is tempted to say, while at the same time remarking on the amazing persistence and tortuous transformations of the philistine spirit in English letters.

The only sympathetic literary relationship Leavis allows Lawrence is one with George Eliot. But surely Lawrence had as much in common with, say, Tolstoy and Nietzsche, as he had with the author of *Middlemarch*. Nor would a reader guess from these lonely embattled pages that anyone besides Leavis had ever written warmly or well about D. H. Lawrence. For all such—and they have been in fact quite numerous—he has one of his small but deadly grenades: "One's tips have been taken up," he writes—meaning, I am afraid, *his* tips—"and have been stultified in the application." In large part, Leavis' own book is stultified by his attempt to appropriate Lawrence for the traditions of "Little England" and for himself as their spokesman.

1956

England Now–
Ariel
or Caliban

Dylan Thomas's radio play, *Under Milk Wood,* is a liquefied Welsh version of Joyce's Dublin Nighttown, with the tears flowing freely and the laughter running over. All of Joyce's buried sentiment, all of his ultimate acquiescence in the lifeness of life, briskly surfaces in *Under Milk Wood,* disports itself in abandon, and cries with Polly Garter, the town fancy-woman of the play, "Oh, isn't life a terrible thing, thank God." No anomalies or contradictions in this Welsh dream-village, no heartbroken mothers, spoiled priests or wandering Jews. Where Joyce, Yeats and others of the older generation had been intense, haunted and hard-working, Thomas was sportive, protean, defiantly untragic. He was Glendower to their Hotspur and could call spirits from the vasty deep by simply raising his voice. Where his elders had strained, he relaxed, although he did so in a medium of language and fancy which they had helped to renew—as it were, for his pleasure. He made a playground of their time-defying and nature-resistant monuments of the literary art, climbing all over those obdurate surfaces and cheerfully de-filing them. He was "the artist as a young dog," according to the title of his volume of autobiographic sketches.

In his radio play, the young dog's tricks include some strik-ing impersonations of his master. *Under Milk Wood* is often slavishly Joycean. "From Beynon Butchers in Coronation Street, the smell of fried liver sidles out with onions on its breath. And listen! In the breakfast room behind the shop, Mr. and Mrs. Beynon, waited upon by their treasure, enjoy, between bites, their everymorning hullabaloo, and Mrs. Beynon slips the gristly bits under the tasseled tablecloth to her fat cat." But Thomas's mimicry here tends to advertise his differences from Joyce. These consist not only in the broader humor of "liver with onions on its breath" and similar flights, but in the charmed ease with which the potential anomalies of existence are turned into jests: Mr. Pugh the would-be wife-poisoner; Mrs. Ogmore-Pritchard with her two husbands, both of them dead; Mrs. Willy-Nilly the postman's wife, "full of tea to her double-chinned brim . . . and always ready to steam open the mail." Then there is the radical loosening of Joyce's austere form, the musical interweaving of the many voices, which transform the sleeping inhabitants of Thomas's Welsh village into pure spirit—or whatever their insubstantial substance is.

Performed by disembodied voices on radio or records, *Under Milk Wood* is all that it sets out to be. The spirits do really come at the poet's call, the act of levitation takes place before the mind's eye. But to stage the work in the regular way—with curtains, costumes and other props—is to risk alerting the doubting Hotspur in a spectator. This an English company recently did in a production of *Under Milk Wood* imported from London to New York. Some fifty players bounced, gestured and hallooed their way through the text, each of them determined to make the most of the brief moments allotted to him on stage. In their efforts to look evanescent they merely succeeded in falling over one another on a set which, with its numerous levels and compartments, was an elaborate trap. The London production brought out the least endearing aspects of the play. Its vapors tended to collect, settle and condense into moist banalities—something that doesn't happen in Thomas's best poems.

Poetry appears to remain Britain's most dependable literary export, for Dylan Thomas has had a greater reputation and influence, in America at least, than any other British-born writer since Auden. The novelists and playwrights of that country get only a passing celebrity here, despite the eagerness of many Americans to enjoy and learn from them. The women come and go talking of C. P. Snow—or Henry Green or Graham Greene or Joyce Cary or Christopher Fry —but not for long. Perhaps Kingsley Amis, John Wain, John Osborne and others of the younger English generation will prove more infectious. They are prose writers, for the most part; they aim to represent what they believe is a more central and more enduring Britain than Thomas represented: the Britain of factories, small shops and provincial universities; and as a group they are said to hold Thomas in some disdain.

Osborne's play, *Look Back in Anger,* while it is famously of this school, seems inferior of its kind to Amis' novel, *Lucky Jim.* Amis' inventiveness in the department of action is not shared by Osborne. What Osborne gives us is only a full-length portrait, quite ambiguous in its implications, of a man raging in the abstract dark of his largely self-spun universe. *Look Back in Anger* is nevertheless well worth contemplating, especially in the excellent production it is getting in New York, where the original London cast is mostly present.

The New York critics were friendly to *Look Back in Anger,* but they did in some cases object that the hero's anger is in sufficiently motivated. It is—by intention, I assume.

Jimmy Porter, as he is called, is that somewhat depressing
figure with which certain American movies and novels, as
well as certain young writers who contribute to symposia on
the problems of their generation, have made us familiar over
here: the rebel without a cause. This creature is more interesting in his English shape. Having wit and rhetoric, Jimmy
makes something, dramatically speaking, of his baseless re-
volt, his career of gratuitous inaction. For his wit and
rhetoric, he is able to draw on a long line of British moral
bullies and railers, from Hamlet to D. H. Lawrence. Politi-
cally impotent though he is, Jimmy Porter can at least blow
his jazz trumpet and search the newspapers for gratifying
instances of scandal and fatuity in caste-bound Britain.
Mainly, he is free to abuse his wife, her family, her social
class, her England. Porter is of working-class origins while
Alison, his wife, belongs to the upper sections of society. As
his "hostage"—her word for it—she helplessly submits to his
accusing tirades. *He* knows things undreamt of in *her* philosophy; *he* has seen, as *she* hasn't, men suffer and die; in short,
he's spiritually alive and *she's* spiritually dead.

Jimmy Porter has Labour Party posters on his wall but
doesn't really envision a changed social order. Failing this,
he tries to make a blood sacrifice of his wife—all his fantasies
are of blood-letting. The trouble, as he sees it, is with his
class enemies even more than with himself. They are all
empty do-nothings like his wife, whom he calls "the Lady
Pusillanimous," and do not even put up a fight. Jimmy rails,
Alison quails; and between them they enact an endless ritual
of mutual damnation in their dreary Midlands flat. Their
windows open on a covered areaway; their door gives on a
hall, a much used bathroom and the quarters of a landlady
who may throw them out at any moment. The furnishings

look provisional, as if waiting for the landlady's ire or a bomb to finish them. Two friends share the Porters' lives for a while without in the long run loosening the pair's mortal embrace. Amid all that is insubstantial in their lives, this grim association alone persists. Meanwhile, Jimmy finds his ideal opponent in his mother-in-law, who never appears in the play. On her imagined presence, embodied in a gas burner downstage, he lavishes his finest flights of abuse, drawing enthusiastically on Hamlet's wit of worms and corpses. Jimmy Porter is often a detestable character from any point of view, including—at moments—the author's. With all its monotony of structure, its false starts into domestic melodrama or screwball comedy, *Look Back in Anger* has the courage of its author's talent for relentless portraiture. There's nothing wrong with Jimmy Porter that a good revolution wouldn't cure, if a good revolution were conceivable by him or anyone else connected with the play. But it isn't. And so a potentially political play becomes—again, I suppose, intentionally—a private lives play of the most suffocating kind. Of such proportions, presumably, is the social stalemate in Great Britain at present that Dylan Thomas can portray an entire community by the simple device of disembodying its inhabitants, whereas John Osborne, for all his socialist concerns, is stuck with a ménage—and *such* a ménage—*à deux*.

1958

Pieces
of the
Hour

Known to professors as essays, to members of the public as articles, and to writers as pieces, works of the kind collected in these three volumes* flourish in the periodicals, big and little, new and old, at the present time. Making us all frenetically magazine-minded, they keep us thumbing through an ever expanding array of publications. When may we expect the piece of the hour in *Organic Gardening*, the indispensable article in *The Yale Review?* And having first enriched the magazine world, many of them achieve a second existence in omnibus volumes such as those at hand. Mr. Vidal's volume is comparatively small. But its acknowledgments page reveals a range of magazine publication which could scarcely be bettered, extending as it does from *Life* to *Zero* The ranges of Mr. Gold and Mr. Swados are pretty impressive too. Roughly averaged, they stretch from *The Hudson Review* to *Playboy*.

Of the three, all in some degree novelists by profession, Gold is the only one who brings to essay writing anything like his full equipment as a writer of novels. Where Swados and Vidal compose essays to persuade us of the validity of their ideas, Gold composes them to show us the meaning of his personal experience.

---

* *Rocking the Boat* by Gore Vidal; *The Age of Happy Problems* by Herbert Gold; *A Radical's America* by Harvey Swados.

Neither effort need exclude the other, of course, and *The Age of Happy Problems* contains several essays that advance ideas on manners and conduct. But even in these reflective pieces Gold draws on memories of dilemmas faced by himself ("Divorce as a Moral Act," "How to Be an Artist's Wife,"), and he writes in a style vaguely suggesting the nervous rhythms of dramatic monologue. But if he tends, as I think, to extract the sweetest wisdom from the bitterest experiences, this is probably a consequence, not of his novelistic approach but of some unworkable partnership between the two chief aspects of his literary personality. One half of him is trying to be a good citizen, a modest hero of moral "commitment." The other half remains a wanderer in the underworld of disgust and despair, doomed to circle back and back over his past as if no moral problem he has encountered was really capable of solution, no city he has visited was ever really strange, and nothing in life was ever quite finished. God knows we are most of us halved in this way, and Gold would be an exemplary essayist if only the citizen and the wanderer were franker with each other and could agree on a common style of writing. As it is, they seem to be involved in a process of mutual intimidation, with the result that one of them sounds compulsively miserable, the other primly sentimental. Neither has a good time; and between the partner who goes in for the fanciest of mandarin prose ("Still, we are not blithe spirits; birds we are not,") and the partner who produces the bleakest of gut prose ("good belly luck," "my battery," meaning his creative energy, "forking up eggs," "I ogle the oglers,") the reader himself has a rough time too.

The best pieces in the book are the portraits of cities that Gold has lived in or visited at some length. His feeling for the modern city and for the oppressed or corrupted lives lived therein is strong. So is his talent for objective reportage—as long as he sticks to it. But as a rule he doesn't stick to it; the inner moodiness takes over. Read in sequence, his metropolitan studies show a certain monotony of grayness in the emotional weather. Scrutinizing his native Cleveland he observes an "acrid pall" hanging above one section of the city. This pall seems to follow the traveler everywhere like a bad conscience. It even trails him to Paris, forbidding him so much as a provisional indulgence in the simple pleasures of escapism. "Death in Miami Beach" is the most brilliant performance in the book. A highly wrought essay-parable, it calls upon all the brutality and vulgarity of the Florida resort city to testify to its theme: the peculiar grimness of death in a mass society. The theme is urgent and Gold tracks it down with a fury of irony that seems more urgent still, sometimes inventing gratuitous horrors. A "nude in plaster" glimpsed briefly outside a resort hotel is imagined to be beckoning obscenely to the crowd and saying, "All aboard, you masturbators." I suggest that if the statue is saying anything it is asking humbly that words not be put in its mouth.

Unable to settle their differences, the moralist and the emotionalist in Gold resort to a kind of obfuscating irony. This irony is the last refuge of the divided soul and it is as familiar today as the divided soul itself is. Considered as a feature of the rhetoric of social criticism, it represents a stock response to the stock properties and catchwords of popular culture. (From "soap operas" to "package deals," the properties and phrases of popculture are just about all accounted for in *The Age of Happy Problems*. Gold's title itself is a sardonic reference to that culture: he remarks that a certain television producer demanded "happy stories about happy people with happy problems.") But the triumph of sentimental irony ensures, I suspect, the defeat of social criticism. The sentimental ironist immobilizes himself along with the abuses he is deploring and makes sad war on sitting ducks. Everything tends to become part of the package deal.

If the chief fault of Herbert Gold's essays is easy ironizing, the *occasional* fault of Harvey Swados's essays is the equally easy rhetoric of sociological expertise. In this, Swados abuses the peculiar authority enjoyed by criticism today through its alliance—or what many suppose to be its alliance—with the social sciences and their techniques of the poll and the survey. Swados writes that it is not "accidental that the only civilized TV programs are presented on Sundays when the average viewer is either sleeping it off or visiting relatives . . ." His point is that the television industry, or at least the capitalist spirit embodied in that industry, is deliberately "degrading" the worker (which is what "average viewer" means in the context) by withholding from him its best programs. But Swados's clairvoyance regarding the worker's Sunday habits seems to me to visit upon the worker a different kind of degradation. Has the worker no alternative to sleeping it off or visiting relatives? Can't he go fishing? Are working class hangovers so much worse than other hangovers that they keep a man in bed all Sunday afternoon and on into the evening, thus depriving him of the civilized programs also available at those times of the day? Has Swados access to some statistical study that he is so knowing? Probably not. Probably he is only going through the motions of the sociological expert.

His regard for logic is rarely as much in doubt as it is in this instance. And his regard for the worker in society, for the meaning of work in general, gives his book its special authority. A professed socialist, he is not very good as a defender of Marxist theory. The essays written from a dogmatic angle for the party press are stunningly innocent of any serious doubts as to the potential rationality of human society. On most other subjects Swados is persuasive. He is good when he is contending against the complacent economics of affluence. His proofs that an authentic working class still exists and suffers are definitive. So are his studies in the malaise consequent upon non-working. As a critic of the intellectual life of America today he manages to be impressively monitory without sounding like a common scold. He doesn't cry "No in Thunder" like Leslie Fiedler and Jove. He is especially good at pointing to the historical roots of "anger," "guilt," "sex," and "self-advertisement" considered as literary staples.

"The Cult of Personality" is his phrase for the self-promoters, and it is a pretty dim phrase at that. Any intellectual tendency can be, and usually is, dismissed as a "cult" by somebody; and what is a "culture" but the sum of its "cults"? Swados's capacity to shape an argument is greater than his capacity to turn a phrase. His words seldom sound as if they belonged to anyone in particular. Perhaps he should join that cult of personality himself. At most he sometimes sounds like a youngish socialist imitating an old socialist who finds himself in polite literary company. "It may be accounted cause for optimism that this play has found an audience"—that sort of thing. But his "Robinson Crusoe—the Man Alone" would be a fine performance in any company. Devoted to demonstrating Defoe's practical humanism, "his ability to normalize the abnormal," the essay also testifies to Swados's similar humanism and abilities.

Gore Vidal would probably be the Third Man in any trio of

modern American writers. We learn why from *Rocking the Boat,* which, like the other two books, is frequently autobiographical. As a youth the writer was exposed to some wealth and much Washington senatorial society; and in his guise as an essayist, just as in his social background, there is a mixture—sometimes disturbing, generally engaging—of dazzle and duty.

Vidal's role is that of the free spirit; and through his devotion to writing and to ideas he has made this risky attitude effectively his own, as distinct from merely owing it to his background. Only occasionally does he appear to be under the necessity of reminding a possibly forgetful world of his privileged state. Then he is apt to sound like some member of Proust's ducal family, the Guermantes. One of the first-rate things in *Rocking the Boat* is a sketch of President Kennedy done from the life and enriched with personal observation. It is "good journalism" with a touch of Plutarchian stateliness. Quite in the Guermantes spirit of self-advertising humility, however, is Vidal's remark apropos the White House: "I am happy to say that I have no influence."

So much for the dazzle; the duty comes out in his attacks on dullness, demagogy, and the injustices done to individuals through the abuse of power by statesmen, literary critics, and cops. Indeed power is Vidal's chief subject, just as work is Swados's. The enjoyment of power interests him as much as does the abuse of it, and in several of his best essays he explores the ways in which possessing it or wanting it have modified the fate of individuals from the Twelve Caesars to Senator Goldwater. His friendly essay on Norman Mailer reminds Mailer that there are some people for whom "the preoccupation with power is a great waste of time."

I don't mean to suggest that power is the sole subject of

Rocking the Boat. A professed satirist just as Mr. Swados is a professed socialist, Vidal fires away at numerous features of American life and letters. Some (but not all) of his best stuff is satirical; for example, his brilliant critique of the slogan-eering use made of love and psychoanalysis on Broadway; or his feud with those writers who have converted the American vernacular into an official literary mode, a "national style." *Rocking the Boat* is even more of a miscellany than *A Radical's America* or *Happy Problems*. It includes things that Vidal has written over the past ten or twelve years while pursuing his various careers as a novelist, a writer for television, the movies, and the stage, and a candidate for political office. His many subjects are touched upon with sharply varying degrees of thoroughness. The book does nevertheless have, besides the recurring concern with power, a distinct unity of tone. And this tone, one of its great attractions, clearly reflects a certain style of being and doing in the author. It arises from an unusual (in our time) conjunction in him of audacity, wit, and pure if spasmodic intelligence. That boat Vidal is cheerfully rocking is a small-scale ship of state. He is testing its ability to float, not all culture and "the family" too, but only a single, separate, rather exacting person like himself. There are, he plainly implies, *other* free spirits besides Gore Vidal. *Rocking the Boat* is further distinguished by a remarkable literary style: clear, unmannered, lively, at times dazzling but never unmindful of its duty to be prose. He prefers to call the writings in *Rocking the Boat* neither essays nor articles nor pieces but "comments."

1962

James
Baldwin and
"The Man"

As a writer of polemical essays on the Negro question James Baldwin has no equals. He probably has, in fact, no real competitors. The literary role he has taken on so deliberately and played with so agile an intelligence is one that no white writer could possibly imitate and that few Negroes, I imagine, would wish to embrace as a whole. Mr. Baldwin is the Negro *in extremis,* a virtuoso of ethnic suffering, defiance and aspiration. His role is that of the man whose complexion constitutes his fate, and not only in a society poisoned by prejudice but, it sometimes seems, in general. For he appears to have received a heavy dose of existentialism; he is at least half-inclined to see the Negro question in the light of the Human Condition. So he wears his color as Hester Prynne did her scarlet letter, proudly. And like her he converts this thing, in itself so absurdly material, into a form of consciousness, a condition of spirit. Believing himself to have been branded as different from and inferior to the white majority, he will make a virtue of his situation. He will *be* different and in his own way be better.

His major essays—for example, those collected in *Notes of a Native Son*—show the extent to which he is able to be different and in his own way better. Most of them were written, as other such pieces generally are, for the magazines, some obviously on assignment. And their subjects—a book, a person, a locale, an encounter—are the inevitable subjects of magazine essays. But Mr. Baldwin's way with them is far from inevitable. To apply criticism "in depth" to *Uncle Tom's Cabin* is, for him, to illuminate not only a book, an author, an age, but a whole strain in the country's culture. Similarly with those routine themes, the Paris expatriate and Life With Father, which he treats in "Equal In Paris" and the title piece of *Notes of a Native Son,* and which he wholly transfigures. Of course the transfiguring process in Baldwin's essays owes something to the fact that the point of view is a Negro's, an outsider's, just as the satire of American manners in *Lolita* and *Morte d'Urban* depends on their being written from the angle of, respectively, a foreign-born creep and a Catholic priest of American birth. But Baldwin's point of view in his essays is not merely that of the generic Negro. It is, as I have said, that of a highly stylized Negro whose language is distinguished by clarity, brevity, and a certain formal elegance. He is in love with syntax, with sentences that mount through clearly articulated stages to a resounding and clarifying climax and then gracefully subside. For instance this one, from *The Fire Next Time:*

> Girls, only slightly older than I was, who sang in the choir or taught Sunday school, the children of holy parents, underwent, before my eyes, their incredible metamorphosis, of which the most bewildering aspect was not their budding breasts or their rounding behinds but something deeper and more subtle, in their eyes, their heat, their odor, and the inflection of their voices.

Nobody else in democratic America writes sentences quite like this anymore. They suggest the ideal prose of an ideal literary community, some aristocratic France of one's dreams. This former Harlem boy has undergone his own incredible metamorphosis.

His latest book, *The Fire Next Time*, differs in important ways from his earlier work in the essay. Its subjects are less concrete, less clearly defined; to a considerable extent he has exchanged criticism for prophecy, analysis for exhortation and the results for his mind and style are in part disturbing. *The Fire Next Time* gets its title from a slave song: "God gave Noah the rainbow sign,/ No more water, the fire next time." But this small book with the incendiary title consists of two independent essays, both in the form of letters. One is a brief affair entitled "My Dungeon Shook" and addressed to "My Nephew on the One Hundredth Anniversary of the Emancipation." The ominous promise of this title is fulfilled in the text. Between the hundred-year-old anniversary and the fifteen-year-old nephew the disparity is too great even for a writer of Baldwin's rhetorical powers. The essay reads like some specimen of "public speech" as practiced by MacLeish or Norman Corwin. It is not good Baldwin.

The other, much longer, much more significant essay appeared first in a pre-Christmas number of *The New Yorker*, where it made, understandably, a sensation. It is called "Down At the Cross: Letter From a Region of My Mind." The subtitle should be noted. Evidently the essay is to be taken as only a partial or provisional declaration on Mr. Baldwin's part, a single piece of his mind. Much of it, however, requires no such appeal for caution on the reader's part. Much of it is unexceptionably first-rate. For example, the reminiscences of the writer's boyhood, which form the lengthy introduction. Other of Baldwin's writings have made us familiar with certain aspects of his Harlem past. Here he

concentrates on quite different things: the boy's increasing
awareness of the abysmally narrow world of choice he inhabits as a Negro, his attempt to escape a criminal existence by
undergoing a religious conversion and becoming at fifteen a
revivalist preacher, his discovery that he must learn to "in-
spire fear" if he hopes to survive the fear inspired in him by
"the man"—the white man.

In these pages we come close to understanding why he
eventually assumed his rather specialized literary role. It
seems to have grown naturally out of his experience of New
York City. As distinct from a rural or small-town Negro boy,
who is early and firmly taught "his place", young Baldwin
knew the treacherous fluidity and anonymity of the metropo-
lis where hidden taboos and unpredictable animosities lay in
wait for him and a trip to the 42nd Street Library could be a
grim adventure. All this part of the book is perfect; and when
Baldwin finally gets to what is his ostensible subject, the
Black Muslims or Nation of Islam movement, he is very good
too. As good, that is, as possible considering that his relations
with the movement seem to have been slight. He once shared
a television program with Malcolm X, "the movement's sec-
ond-in-command," and he paid a brief and inconclusive visit
to the first-in-command, the Honorable Elijah Muhammad
and his entourage at the party's headquarters in Chicago.
(Muhammad ranks as a prophet; to him the Black Muslim
doctrines were "revealed by Allah Himself.") Baldwin reports the Chicago encounter in charming detail and with
what looks like complete honesty. On his leaving the party's
rather grand quarters, the leader insisted on providing him
with a car and driver to protect him "from the white devils
until he gets wherever it is he is going." Baldwin accepted,
he tells us, adding wryly: "I was, in fact, going to have a

drink with several white devils on the other side of town."

He offers some data on the Black Muslim movement, its aims and finances. But he did a minimum of homework here. Had he done more he might at least have provided a solid base for the speculative fireworks the book abounds in. To cope thoroughly with the fireworks in short space, or perhaps any space, seems impossible. Ideas shoot from the book's pages as the sparks fly upward, in bewildering quantity and at random. I don't mean that it is all fireworks. On the cruel paradoxes of the Negro's life, the failures of Christianity, the relations of Negro and Jew, Baldwin is superb. But a lot of damage is done to his argument by his indiscriminate raids on Freud, Lawrence, Sartre, Genet and other psychologists, metaphysicians and melodramatists. Still more damage is done by his refusal to draw on anyone so humble as Martin Luther King and his fellow-practitioners of non-violent struggle.

For example: "White Americans do not believe in death, and this is why the darkness of my skin so intimidates them." But suppose one or two white Americans are *not* intimidated. Suppose someone coolly asks what it means to "believe in death." Again: "Do I really *want* to be integrated into a burning house?" Since you have no other, yes; and the better-disposed firemen will welcome your assistance. Again: "A vast amount of the energy that goes into what we call the Negro problem is produced by the white man's profound desire not to be judged by those who are not white." You exaggerate the white man's consciousness of the Negro. Again: "The real reason that non-violence is considered to be a virtue in Negroes . . . is that white men do not want their lives, their self-image, or their property threatened." Of course they don't, especially their lives. Moreover, this imputing of "real reasons" for the behavior of entire populations is self-defeating, to put it mildly. One last quotation, this time a regular apocalypse:

> In order to survive as a human, moving, moral weight in the world, America and all the Western nations will be forced to re-examine themselves and release themselves from many things that are now taken to be sacred, and to discard nearly all the assumptions that have been used to justify their lives and their anguish and their crimes so long.

Since whole cultures have never been known to "discard nearly all their assumptions" and yet remain intact, this amounts to saying that any essential improvement in Negro-white relations, and thus in the quality of American life, is unlikely.

So much for the fireworks. What damage, as I called it, do they do to the writer and his cause—which is also the concern of plenty of others? When Baldwin replaces criticism with prophecy, he manifestly weakens his grasp of his role, his style, and his great theme itself. And to what end? Who is likely to be moved by such arguments, unless it is the more literate Black Muslims, whose program Baldwin specifically rejects as both vindictive and unworkable. And with the situation as it is in Mississippi and elsewhere—dangerous, that is, to the Negro struggle and the whole social order—is not a writer of Baldwin's standing obliged to submit his assertions to some kind of pragmatic test, some process whereby their truth or untruth will be gauged according to their social utility? He writes: "The Negroes of this country may never be able to rise to power, but they are very well placed indeed to precipitate chaos and ring down the curtain on the American dream." I should think that the anti-Negro extremists were even better placed than the Negroes to precipitate chaos, or at least to cause a lot of trouble; and it is unclear to me how *The Fire Next Time,* in its madder moments, can do anything except inflame the former and confuse the latter.

1963